T0384347

Investment Pattern of LICI and Select Private LICs in the Post-reforms Era in India

Shib Pada Patra · Siddhartha Sankar Saha ·
Mitrendu Narayan Roy

Investment Pattern of LICI and Select Private LICs in the Post-reforms Era in India

palgrave
macmillan

Shib Pada Patra
Department of Commerce
Chittaranjan College
Kolkata, West Bengal, India

Mitrendu Narayan Roy
Department of Commerce
Goenka College of Commerce
and Business Administration
Kolkata, West Bengal, India

Siddhartha Sankar Saha
Department of Commerce
Faculty Council for Post Graduate
Studies in Commerce, Social Welfare
and Business Management
University of Calcutta
Kolkata, West Bengal, India

ISBN 978-981-19-2798-0   ISBN 978-981-19-2799-7   (eBook)
https://doi.org/10.1007/978-981-19-2799-7

Cover illustration: © Melisa Hasan

This Palgrave Macmillan imprint is published by the registered company Springer Nature Singapore Pte Ltd.
The registered company address is: 152 Beach Road, #21-01/04 Gateway East, Singapore 189721, Singapore

PREFACE

The idea of the present research-oriented reference book on *Investment Pattern of LICI and Select Private LICs in the Post-reforms Era in India* has been developed out of a lively discussion with the authors. Development of the life insurance industry, which is an important part of the financial system, accelerates capital accumulation and leads the domestic savings towards sectorial investments. In fact, life insurance companies in India are very significant financial institutions for mobilising savings from household sectors of the economy and play a significant role in channelling this savings from surplus sectors to deficit sectors for the productive purposes. At present, one public and 23 private life insurance companies are operating in India. The Insurance Regulatory and Development Authority of India (IRDAI) regulates the savings mobilisation and investment portfolio of life insurance companies. In this backdrop, this is momentous to analyse the investment portfolio of public and select private life insurance in India.

Dr. Shib Pada Patra, the first author of the book, conveys his sincere gratitude to his research mentor, Professor (Dr.) Siddhartha Sankar Saha, Professor of Commerce, Department of Commerce, University of Calcutta, Kolkata, India, who kindly consented to be the second author of the book for his valuable guidance and constant support during the research work. The first author would like to convey his deep sense of gratitude in great reverence; to him without his inspiration and valuable advice, this present research work would not have been completed.

Moreover, the first author is also thankful to the third author of the book, Dr. Mitrendu Narayan Roy, Assistant Professor, Goenka College of Commerce and Business Administration, Kolkata, India, for extending his gracious assistance with respect to the technical as well as logistic matters of the book publication. He has made an endeavour to connect with the publisher for every correspondence.

The authors are pleased to put on record best regards to the reverend teachers in the area of business and finance in India for their valuable advices. The authors owe their gratitude to the learned authors of India and abroad from whose work the authors have taken different ideas for their present research work. The authors acknowledge with thanks the guidance given by different learned authors on the contemporary issues for the research study.

The authors convey their thanks to numerous friends for their support and cooperation. They are also grateful to the librarians and the staff members of the Central Library of University of Calcutta and Bidhan Chandra Roy Memorial Library of Indian Institute of Management (IIM), Calcutta, for allowing them to use their valuable books, periodicals, journals and other documents for the present research work. There is no language to express gratitude to the parents of the authors for their blessings to complete the research work.

Finally, the authors would like to put on record their sincere thanks to the publisher, Palgrave Macmillan, especially its editorial team comprising Ms. Tula Weis, Ms. Sandeep Kaur, Ms. Carolyn Zhand and Mr. Anand Kumar Mariappan for their seamless cooperation in the publishing process.

Kolkata, India
July 2022

Dr. Shib Pada Patra
Professor (Dr.) Siddhartha Sankar Saha
Dr. Mitrendu Narayan Roy

CONTENTS

1 **Introduction**   1
  1.1 *Background of the Research*   2
  1.2 *Statement of the Research Problem*   4
  1.3 *Research Questions*   5
  1.4 *Review of Literature*   5
  1.5 *Objectives of the Study*   12
  1.6 *Research Methodology*   12
  1.7 *Limitations of the Study*   15
  1.8 *The Scheme of Work*   15
  References   16

2 **Evolution and Regulatory Framework of Life Insurance
  Companies in India: A Conceptual Review**   19
  2.1 *Introduction*   20
  2.2 *Evolution of Life Insurance Industry*   20
  2.3 *Overview of Life Insurance Companies Operating
       in India*   28
  2.4 *Regulatory Framework Governing Life Insurance
       Business*   28
  2.5 *Investment Portfolio of Life Insurance Industry*   55
  2.6 *Conclusion*   64
  References   66

3   Premium Mobilisation and Investment Portfolio
    by the LICI and Select Private Life Insurance
    Companies: An Analytical Study   69
    3.1   Introduction   70
    3.2   Objectives   70
    3.3   Methodology   71
    3.4   Analysis and Findings   72
    3.5   Conclusion   104
    References   106

4   An Empirical Insight into the Premium Mobilisation
    and Investment Portfolio of the LICI and Select
    Private Life Insurance Companies in India   107
    4.1   Introduction   108
    4.2   Objectives of the Study   108
    4.3   Research Methods   109
    4.4   Analysis and Discussion   110
    References   155

5   Concluding Observations and Suggestions   157
    5.1   Introduction   158
    5.2   Summary of Major Findings in Previous Chapters   158
    5.3   Economic and Social Implications: A Few Suggestions   164
    5.4   Areas of Further Research   165
    5.5   Conclusions   166

Bibliography   169
Index   177

About the Authors

 **Dr. Shib Pada Patra** is an Assistant Professor of Commerce, Chittaranjan College, Kolkata (West Bengal), India, since July 2008, teaching undergraduate students. He did his post-graduation in commerce from the University of Calcutta in 1996 and qualified SLET under UGC in 2000. He obtained his Ph.D. from Department of Commerce, University of Calcutta, under the supervision of Dr. Siddhartha Sankar Saha in 2019. He has presented a number of research papers in several national and international conferences and published around 6 research papers in journals of national and international repute.

Professor (Dr.) Siddhartha Sankar Saha is Head and a Professor of Commerce, Department of Commerce, University of Calcutta, Kolkata (West Bengal), India. He became Dean, Faculty Council for Post-graduate Studies in Commerce, Social Welfare and Business Management, University of Calcutta. He was a member in Senate and Syndicate, University of Calcutta. He was also Director, University of Calcutta—Calcutta Stock Exchange Centre of Excellence in Financial Market (CUCSE—CEFM), and Internal Quality Assurance Cell (IQAC), University of Calcutta. Previously, he had served Department of Commerce (Accounting and Finance), St. Xavier's College (Autonomous), Kolkata, India, for several years. He obtained his Ph.D. in Finance from the Department of Commerce, University of Calcutta. He has more than two decades of teaching experience at undergraduate and postgraduate levels in accounting, finance and control in universities and business schools, and is presently supervising a number of M.Phil. and Ph.D. scholars. He has completed two Major Research Project (MRP) funded by the UGC, New Delhi, India, and by the ICSSR, New Delhi, India. He has more than 131 research papers to his credit in journals of national and international repute, conference proceedings of national and international conferences and edited volumes. He has also been invited to chair sessions and deliver keynote speeches at many international conferences in India and abroad. He has become a prolific author and has contributed 12 books in the field of finance published by publication houses of national and international repute, such as McGraw-Hill Education, Taxmann, LAP

Lambert Academic Publishing, Scholars' Press, Emerald Publishing and Palgrave-Macmillan (Springer).

Dr. Mitrendu Narayan Roy is an Assistant Professor of Commerce, Goenka College of Commerce and Business Administration (West Bengal), India, since May 2015, teaching at both undergraduate and post-graduate levels. He did his post-graduation in commerce from the University of Calcutta in 2010 and qualified NET with JRF under UGC in 2011. He obtained his Ph.D. from Department of Commerce, University of Calcutta, under the supervision of Professor (Dr.) Siddhartha Sankar Saha in 2016. He has presented a number of research papers in several national and international conferences and published more than 34 research papers in journals of national and international repute. Currently, he has become a co-author of two research-oriented books in the field of finance published by Emerald Publishing Ltd., UK, and Palgrave-Macmillan (Springer).

ABBREVIATIONS

ADF	Augmented Dickey-Fuller
AI	Approved Investment
ANOVA	Analysis of Variance
AS	Accounting Standard
BAJAJ	Bajaj Allianz Life Insurance Company Ltd.
BIRLA	Birla Sun Life Insurance Company Ltd.
CAGR	Compound Annual Growth Rate
DEA	Data Envelopment Analysis
DF	Degree of Freedom
DV	Dependent Variable
GDP	Gross Domestic Product
GICI	General Insurance Corporation of India
HDFC	HDFC Standard Life Insurance Company Ltd.
HSD	Honestly Significant Difference
ICAI	Institute of Chartered Accountants of India
ICICI	ICICI−Prudential Life Insurance Company Ltd.
II	Infrastructure Investment
IPO	Initial Public Offer
IRDAI	Insurance Regulatory and Development Authority of India
IV	Independent Variable
K-W	Kruskal-Wallis
LICI	Life Insurance Corporation of India
MAX	Max Life Insurance Company Ltd.
MLRA	Multiple Linear Regression Analysis
M-W	Mann-Whitney
OAI	Other than Approved Investment

OYH	Own Your Home
PC	Premium Collection
PLIC	Private Life Insurance Company
RBI	Reserve Bank of India
SBI	SBI Life Insurance Company Ltd.
SD	Standard Deviation
SE	Standard Error
SEBI	Securities and Exchange Board of India
SFA	Stochastic Frontier Analysis
SS	Sum of Squares
S-W	Shapiro-Wilks
TI	Total Investment
ULIP	Unit Linked Product
USA	United States of America
UTI	Unit Trust of India

Standard Measures/Symbols

H_0	Null Hypothesis
H_1	Alternative Hypothesis
R^2	Strength of Association
r	Pearson's Correlation Coefficient
Log	Natural Logarithm
P-Value	Probability Value
β_i	Estimated Coefficient for 'i' the Variable
$\overline{X}$	Mean Value of a Variable
$\hat{\beta}$	Estimated Value of Coefficient
$\sum$	Summation
U	Test Statistic of M-W Test
H	Test Statistic of K-W Test
$\widetilde{Y_i}.$	Median of a Variable
W	Test Statistic of S-W Test

LIST OF CHARTS

Chart 3.1   Growth of total premium collection (*Source* Compiled based on Table 3.2 using MS Excel)   74

Chart 3.2   Growth in Total Investment (*Source* Compiled based on Table 3.4 using MS Excel)   76

Chart 3.3   Growth of investment in government and other approved securities (*Source* Compiled based on Table 3.6 using MS Excel)   78

Chart 3.4   Growth of infrastructure investment (*Source* Compiled based on Table 3.8 using MS Excel)   80

Chart 3.5   Growth of approved investment (*Source* Compiled based on Table 3.10 using MS Excel)   83

Chart 3.6   Growth of other than approved investment (*Source* Compiled based on Table 3.12 using MS Excel)   85

Chart 3.7   Trend of total premium collection (*Source* Table 3.13)   88

Chart 3.8   Trend of total investment (*Source* Table 3.14)   90

Chart 3.9   Trend in investment in government and other approved securities (*Source* Table 3.15)   92

Chart 3.10   Trend in infrastructure investment (*Source* Table 3.16)   94

Chart 3.11   Trend in approved investment (*Source* Table 3.17)   96

Chart 3.12   Trend in other than approved investments (*Source* Table 3.18)   98

LIST OF TABLES

Table 2.1	Products and offices of Indian life insurers	29
Table 2.2	Brief overview of life insurance companies	30
Table 2.3	Regulations in the pre-independence era	40
Table 2.4	Select regulations during nationalisation	44
Table 2.5	Regulations issued during reforms phase	48
Table 2.6	Regulations issued in the post-reforms era	51
Table 2.7	Investment portfolio in the pre-independence era	56
Table 2.8	Investment portfolio during nationalisation	57
Table 2.9	Investment policy of the LICI in the post-nationalisation era	59
Table 2.10	Investment portfolio of life fund	64
Table 2.11	Investment portfolio of pension and annuity fund	65
Table 2.12	Investment portfolio of ULIP fund	65
Table 3.1	Total premium collection (As on 31st March) (Rs. in Crores)	73
Table 3.2	Growth in total premium collection (%)	74
Table 3.3	Total Investment (As on 31st March) (Rs. in Crores)	75
Table 3.4	Growth in total investment (%)	76
Table 3.5	Investment in government and other approved securities (As on 31st March) (Rs. in Crores)	77
Table 3.6	Growth of investment in government and other approved securities (%)	78
Table 3.7	Infrastructure Investment (As on 31st March) (Rs. in Crores)	79
Table 3.8	Growth of infrastructure investment (%)	80

Table 3.9   Approved Investment (As on 31st March)
             (Rs. in Crores)   82
Table 3.10   Growth of approved investment (%)   83
Table 3.11   Other than approved investment (As on 31st March)
             (Rs. in Crores)   84
Table 3.12   Growth of other than approved investment (%)   84
Table 3.13   Trend in total premium collection (As on 31st March)
             (Rs. in Crores)   87
Table 3.14   Trend in total investment (As on 31st March)
             (Rs. in Crores)   89
Table 3.15   Trend in investment in government and other approved
             securities (As on 31st March) (Rs. in Crores)   91
Table 3.16   Trend in infrastructure investment (As on 31st March)
             (Rs. in Crores)   93
Table 3.17   Trend in approved investment (As on 31st March)
             (Rs. in Crores)   95
Table 3.18   Trend in other than approved investments (As on 31st
             March) (Rs. in Crores)   97
Table 3.19   Correlation between premium collection and total
             investment   99
Table 3.20   Correlation among life insurance companies in terms
             of premium collection   100
Table 3.21   Correlation among life insurance companies in terms
             of total investments   101
Table 3.22   Correlation among life insurance companies in terms
             of investments in IGOAS   102
Table 3.23   Correlation among select life insurance companies
             in terms of II   102
Table 3.24   Correlation among select life insurance companies
             in terms of AI   103
Table 3.25   Correlation among select life insurance companies
             in terms of OAI   105
Table 4.1   Results of S-W test   112
Table 4.2   Results of Levene's test   115
Table 4.3   Results of Welch test   116
Table 4.4   Results of K-W test   118
Table 4.5   Companies with Significant Pair-wise Difference (PC)   119
Table 4.6   Homogenous subsets among life insurers (PC)   119
Table 4.7   Companies with significant pair-wise difference (IGOAS) 120
Table 4.8   Homogenous subsets among life insurers (IGOAS)   120
Table 4.9   Companies with Significant Pair-wise Difference (AI)   121
Table 4.10   Homogenous subsets among life insurers (AI)   121

Table 4.11   Companies with significant pair-wise difference (TI)   122
Table 4.12   Homogenous subsets among life insurers (TI)   123
Table 4.13   Companies with significant pair-wise difference (II)   123
Table 4.14   Homogenous subsets among life insurers (II)   124
Table 4.15   Companies with significant pair-wise difference (OAI)   124
Table 4.16   Homogenous subsets among life insurers (OAI)   124
Table 4.17   Results of Shapiro Wilk's test (impact of recession on PC)   126
Table 4.18   Results of Levene's test (impact of recession on PC)   127
Table 4.19   Results of t-test (impact of recession on PC)   128
Table 4.20   Results of Shapiro Wilk's test (impact of recession on TI)   130
Table 4.21   Results of Levene's test (impact of recession on TI)   131
Table 4.22   Results of t-test (impact of recession on TI)   131
Table 4.23   Results of M-W test (impact of recession on TI)   132
Table 4.24   Results of Shapiro Wilk's test (impact of recession on IGOAS)   134
Table 4.25   Results of Levene's test (impact of recession on IGOAS)   135
Table 4.26   Results of t-test (impact of recession on IGOAS)   135
Table 4.27   Results of Shapiro Wilk's test (impact of recession on II)   136
Table 4.28   Results of Levene's test (impact of recession on II)   137
Table 4.29   Results of t-test (impact of recession on II)   138
Table 4.30   Results of Shapiro Wilk's test (impact of recession on AI)   139
Table 4.31   Results of Levene's test (impact of recession on AI)   140
Table 4.32   Results of t-test (impact of recession on AI)   141
Table 4.33   Results of Shapiro Wilk's test (impact of recession on OAI)   142
Table 4.34   Results of Levene's test (impact of recession on OAI)   143
Table 4.35   Results of t-test (impact of recession on OAI)   144
Table 4.36   Results of Shapiro Wilk's test (impact of ownership structure on select parameters)   145
Table 4.37   Results of Levene's test (impact of ownership structure on select parameters)   146
Table 4.38   Results of t-test (impact of ownership structure on select parameters)   147
Table 4.39   Relationship between company performance and industry performance with respect to select parameters   149
Table 4.40   Impact of company performance on industry performance with respect to select parameters   151

Table 4.41   Strength of association between company performance and industry performance with respect to select parameters   153

Table 4.42   Significance of the strength of association   154

CHAPTER 1

Introduction

Abstract Life insurance companies in India play an important role in Indian financial system in mobilising small savings in the form of life insurance premium from Indian household sectors and investing it in Indian financial market. Life insurance companies accumulate the premium through traditional as well as Unit Linked Products (ULIPs) and mobilise the same into different productive channels. The Insurance Regulatory and Development Authority of India (IRDAI) has mandated the proportion in which the total investible fund can be allocated among different sectors for the purpose of investment. Such mandate by the IRDAI is aimed at return optimisation and safety and security of the fund to meet the policyholders' claim and other operating expenses on the one hand, and achieve larger economic development and social interest on the other. Accordingly, total premium mobilisation is allocated among the following investments: (a) Investment in Government and Other Approved Securities (IGOAS); (b) Infrastructure Investment (II); (c) Approved Investment (AI); and (d) Other than Approved Investment (OAI). Chapter 1, the introductory one, sets the foundation of the overall research that seeks to find out the performance of the Life Insurance Corporation of India Ltd. (LICI) and select private life insurers in terms of their premium mobilisation and sectorial investments. In view of this, the current chapter identifies a specific research problem and points out a few research questions based on research philosophy. Existing literature

S. P. Patra et al., *Investment Pattern of LICI and Select Private LICs
in the Post-reforms Era in India*,
https://doi.org/10.1007/978-981-19-2799-7_1

1

in the related area are reviewed, and the gap in existing researches is identified facilitating formulation of the study objectives, which are addressed
in the subsequent chapters. In order to meet those objectives, a comprehensive chapter-wise methodology has been made and a chapter plan has
been made as well.

Keywords LICI · IGOAS · II · AI · OAI · Premium Mobilisation ·
Total Investment · Sectorial Investment · IRDAI

1.1   Background of the Research

Financial system in a country provides the mechanism for formation of
capital in order to bring development in the economy. It comprises a set
of sub-systems of financial institution, financial market, financial instru-
ment and service and its regulatory bodies through which savings are
transformed into investment. It plays a significant role to mobilise the
surplus funds from surplus sectors to deficit sectors and utilises them
effectively for productive purposes. The level and growth of savings,
investment and capital formation are essential in an economy. The main
function of financial institution and intermediaries operating in the financial system is considered very important. Financial institutions facilitate
the process of capital accumulation by transferring resources from the
savers to investors. Investment institutions have occupied important place
in the well-integrated structure of financial institution. Those institutions are: Life Insurance Corporation of India (LICI), Unit Trust of
India (UTI), General Insurance Corporation of India (GICI), etc. In
this backdrop, development of insurance industry, which is an important
part of the financial system, accelerates capital accumulation and leads the
domestic savings into investment. The insurance sector is an important
component of the financial system in meeting the demand for savings
and in bringing together investors by creating appropriate funding possi-
bility. Therefore, they play an appropriate role in the conversion of savings
into investment (Ege & Bahadir, 2011). Though the insurance company
primarily was engaged in providing insurance to the people, insurance
companies mobilise huge sums by way of insurance premium. There are
two types of insurance. These are: (a) life insurance and (b) general insurance. Life insurance protects an individual and /or his/ her family at the

premature death or at the old age by providing an adequate amount. Life insurance has historically been an important method through which individuals with relatively low incomes have been able to save and invest effectively for the longer period (Dickinson, 2011). Insurance companies collect small amount on a regular basis from a large proportion of the population by designing relatively simple life insurance and savings contracts. With this mechanism, they have been able to accumulate large amount of money. By pooling these savings from many small investors into large accumulations of investable funds, life insurance companies have been able to invest not only in a wider range of investment than individuals would have been able to invest in directly by themselves but have also been able to invest in larger scale and in more risky investment opportunities, which are more beneficial to the economy (Dickinson, 2011). Thus, life insurance is a major device for the mobilisation of the savings of people, which are thereafter channelised into investment in the economy.

In 1956, the life insurance business was nationalised and a single monolithic organisation: The Life Insurance Corporation of India (LICI) was established under the Life Insurance Corporation of India Act, 1956. Nationalisation of life insurance was a further step in the direction of more effective mobilisation of the people's savings (Kumar, 1991). In course of undertaking life insurance business, the LICI mobilises savings of the masses and employs them as investment in various types of securities under different sectors. Recently, the life insurance sector has been opened to the private sector and monitored under a single authority—'Insurance Regulatory and Development Authority of India' (IRDAI), which regulates the entire insurance industry. The parliament passed the IRDA Act, in 1999, and it was incorporated as an autonomous body in April 2000. Currently, there are 24 life insurance companies (both public and private) operating in India. The most significant life insurance companies comprise the LICI and some private life insurance companies including ICICI Prudential, Kotak Mahindra, SBI Life, MetLife, Bajaj Allianz, Sahara India and Aegon Religare. In India, both public and private life insurance companies have built up investment portfolio in a significant magnitude as per IRDA Regulations. Thus, with a view to safeguarding the interests of the policyholders as well as the interest of whole economy, the funds at the disposal of life insurance companies are invested subject to Government Regulations. The IRDAI has issued investment regulations for life insurance companies in 2001. It is noted that investment in Government and other approved securities is not less than 50% of the controlled funds, and the remaining portions are distributed over: (a) infrastructure sector; (b) social sector including rural sector; (c) investment in securities of all India financial institutions; (d) deposits with banks; (e) commercial paper; (f) treasury bills; and (g) approved investments under Sect. 27A of IRDA Regulations (IRDA, 2001). By this portfolio of investment, 24 life insurance companies play a vital role to develop the Indian economy.

1.2   STATEMENT OF THE RESEARCH PROBLEM

Life insurance organisations in India are very important financial institutions in Indian financial system in order to mobilise insurance premium collected from the household sectors into investment in Indian financial market. It is historically an important investment system for a long period. In fact, life insurance companies collect the premium through traditional products as well as Unit Linked Products (ULIPs) and mobilise this premium into different investment instruments of different sectors. As per the IRDA Regulations, investment is made in different sectors on the basis of a portfolio to serve larger economic development and social interest by optimising the return on investment and safety and security of the funds to meet the claims of the policyholders and other expenses to run the life insurance business. The sectorial investments are Investment in Government and Other Approved Securities (IGOAS), Infrastructure Investment (II), Approved Investment (AI) and Other than Approved Investment (OAI). As per IRDAI latest Annual Report 2013–2014, India had secured 11th rank among the 88 countries in life insurance business. India's share was 2% in global insurance market in 2013. In India, life insurance premium collection was Rs. 314,283 crore during 2013–2014. Market share of the LICI had been increased from 72.70% in 2012–2013 to 75.39% in 2013–2014, and it had decreased from 27.30% in 2012–2013 to 24.61% in 2013–2014 for the private life insurance business. Total investment portfolio of life insurers in India was Rs. 1,744,894 crore in 2012–2013 and Rs.1957466 crore in 2013–2014 (IRDAI, 2014). This development of life insurance sector was reflected through life insurance penetration (41.00 USD in 2013) and life insurance density (3.10% in 2013) in India. The IRDAI had prescribed the investment portfolio as per the IRDA (Investment) (Fifth Amendment) Regulations, 2013, and this was maintained by all public and private life insurance companies in India. Therefore, enormous amount of premium collected by public as well as private life insurance companies is invested into different sectors as per the investment portfolio. In this backdrop, the present study, as such, aspires to make a comparative study on investment portfolio of the LICI and select private life insurance companies in India in order to address the current research problem.

1.3 RESEARCH QUESTIONS

Keeping in mind the research problem of the study, the following relevant research questions are emerged out in order to conduct a thorough research study on investment portfolio of the LICI and select private life insurance companies empirically:

(a) What is the trend of insurance premium mobilisation and investment portfolio of the LICI and select major private life insurance companies in the post-reforms era?

(b) What is the comparative relationship among the LICI and select private life insurance companies in India with regard to their insurance premium mobilisation and investment portfolio?

(c) How the LICI and select major private life insurance companies influence life insurance industry in terms of premium mobilisation and investment portfolio?

1.4 REVIEW OF LITERATURE

In order to address those research questions, a survey of literature concerning insurance premium mobilisation and investment portfolio of life insurance companies has been conducted thoroughly. A few of them are enumerated below:

1.4.1 *International Studies*

1.4.1.1 *Pre-Reforms Era*
Horton and Macve (1998) studied the impact of life insurance companies on stock market. It was observed that there was no immediate impact of the LICI on stock markets. Product marketing and organisational efficiency were principal to success of the LICI. Henebry and Diamond (1998) in their paper analysed investment portfolio of 54 life insurance

companies in the USA. The analysis was made on bonds, mortgage, real estate, stocks and other investment. Results of liner regression verified that changes in bond and real estate were not significant, but it was significant in mortgage, stocks and other investment. Results of F-test showed the significant variation between different groups of investment.

1.4.1.2   Post-Reforms Era

Adams and Hardwick (2003) examined annually reported surplus reinsurance, output mix, organisational form and firm size of life insurance firms in the UK. Linear regression analysis explained that higher reinsurance to premium ratio supported higher annual surplus. In this analysis, output mix and firm size were significant determinant of reported annual surplus. Plantin and Rochet (2007) in their book made an economic analysis on the role and design of prudential regulations. Causes of financially distressed insurers and regulations of insurance business were discussed in it. Skipper and Jean (2007) in their book reviewed risk management and insurance in global economy. Economic foundations of insurance, nature and importance of insurance policies had been discussed. The authors also cited the financial services, integration, reinsurance, regulations and taxation in insurance companies.

1.4.1.3   Post-Recession Era

Saad and Idris (2011) analysed efficiency and technical changes in 11 life insurance companies in Malaysia and Brunei. Data Envelopment Analysis (DEA) explored the technical efficiency and efficiency change to the total productivity in insurance sector. Size of the company significantly affected the efficiency change. Koijen and Yogo (2013) analysed the cost of financial friction for life insurers. The study estimated the model of insurance pricing. Net equity inflow was calculated as capital plus surplus minus stockholder's dividend paid. Lee, Lee and Chiu (2013) verified association between life insurance activities and economic growth. Seemingly unrelated, Augmented Dickey-Fuller (ADF) test found a positive relationship between economic activity and growth of life insurance market. Results of F-test indicated that high level of economic growth led higher level of premium income and vice versa. Mahdzan and Victorian (2013) investigated on the determinants of life insurance demand among policyholders in five life insurance companies in Kuala Lumpur, Malaysia. Multiple regression analysis verified that socio-demographic, savings motives, and financial literacy influenced the demand of life insurance business. One-way ANOVA explained significant difference among the groups.

1.4.2   National Studies

1.4.2.1   Pre-Reforms Era

Niwata (1971) in his book highlighted an economic theory for welfare work and social security in business. Here, the author described the insurance companies working on welfare wages and social security in their businesses signifying very important for lower income earner. Kumar (1991) in his book edited the history of insurance and modification of the Insurance Act and regulations in India. Insurance Act, 1938, nationalisation of insurance, policy of life insurance business, and investment and growth statistics of life insurance business were discussed in detail.

1.4.2.2   Post-Reforms Era

Palande, Shah and Lunawat (2003) in their book analysed changing policy and emerging opportunity of the LICI. The book explained the special position of insurance sector in Indian economy, influence of global market, growth and development of Indian insurance industry. Gupta (2003) in his book discussed the future prospect of insurance industry. The author also discussed the future development of life insurance business in India. Bhole (2004) in his book discussed about the life insurance businesses in India. The growth of life insurance business and its different funds, structure of insurance plan and investment portfolio were also mentioned. Desai (2005) in his book mentioned about the financial system and its development process. Life and non-life insurance company, insurance market penetration, investment policy and industrial growth were also explained in the book. Pathak (2006) explained history and development of insurance in Indian financial system. Reforms in insurance sector, portfolio of investment and fund-wise life insurance investment were also discussed. Khan (2006) in his book discussed about the insurance organisation in Indian financial system. The author explained the investment norms and maintenance of books of accounts in Indian insurance companies. Upadhyay and Shrivastawa (2007) in their book highlighted risk management in banking and insurance. Maximising shareholders' return, new accounting framework in insurance industry and history of insurance were discussed in the book. Bhasin (2007) in his book explained the banking and financial market in India during 1947–2007. Nationalisation of life insurance and its development during post-liberalisation were also mentioned in the book. Das and Mohanty (2008) analysed the behaviour of investors on the basis of their age, qualification and profession for the selection of investment in mutual fund or life insurance schemes. Results of two-way ANOVA inferred significant difference in the pattern of investment with respect to age, education and profession. Results of z-test showed domination of men in all the investment avenues as compared to women. Rajendran and Natarajan (2009) in their paper empirically analysed the performance of the LICI during pre- and post-LPG (liberalisation, privatisation and globalisation) as well as volume of competition faced by the LICI. Trend analysis using method of least squares showed that life insurance business was increasing in India and outside and reforms had positive impact on the performance of business of the LICI. Balachandran (2009) in his book talked about life insurance and its business in India. The author highlighted principle of insurance, calculation of premium, Insurance Act and regulations of insurance business.

1.4.2.3   *Post-Recession Era*
Chandra and Ramesh (2011) in their paper analysed lapsing of life insurance policies and its consequences in life insurance sector in India. Result of F-test showed significant influence of age group, policy type and agency on duration of policy. Lapsing of life insurance policies had affected the growth of life insurance business. Bedi and Singh (2011) studied the overall performance of life insurance industry during pre- and post-economic recession era and investment strategy of the LIC over the period 1980–2009 and competition faced by the LICI. The results of F-test revealed that premium collection of the LICI out of total premium collection was decreased for increasing competition from the private sector. Results of t-test and F-test indicated no significant changes in investment pattern over the period 1980 to 2009. Haridas (2011) in his book explained the development of life insurance business in India. Life insurance in India, insurance service, its growth and origin as well as micro-insurance were cited in the book. Negi and Singh (2012) studied the demographic profile of customers of life insurance in Uttarakhand to determine the factors influencing purchase of life insurance products in India. Results of F-test showed significant difference among investors in terms of product quality, brand image, service quality,

customer friendliness, brand loyalty, and commitment. Mean rating of commitment, product quality and brand image, and service quality were higher among males as compared to females. Kumar and Kumari (2012) evaluated the comparative performance of public and private life insurance companies in India. The LICI captured majority of market share, but growth rate of total premium of private life insurance companies was higher as compared to the LICI. Gour and Gupta (2012) studied solvency margin and solvency ratio of five life insurance companies in Indian life insurance sector. On the basis of solvency ratio, ICICI maintained first rank followed by LICI, HDFC, BIRLA and SBI. Noronh and Shiende (2012) in their study measured the cost efficiency scores in public and private life insurance companies. It was observed that the LICI is cost efficient, but private life insurance companies had inconsistent cost efficiency scores. Satpathy and Sahoo (2012) made a comparative discussion on different insurance sectors. It was observed that organisation members were the driving force in insurance business. Panda and Panda (2012) studied the investment decision taken out of insurance investment and mutual fund investment schemes as well as behavioural pattern of the investors. The results of t-test revealed that investors wanted to invest in insurance fund rather than the stock market. While return on mutual funds was more, mutual fund investments were more risky than investment in insurance company. Rai and Medha (2013) in their paper studied determination of the factors and its relative importance to form the customer loyalty in life insurance industry. Multiple regression analysis showed that service quality was an important factor to achieve customer's loyalty. The significant difference between public and private life insurance companies for customers' loyalty was verified using t-test. Saha (2013) in his book discussed about the Indian insurance industry. The author discussed about different products of life insurance business, its regulatory framework and investment portfolio. Padhi (2013) studied the role and performance of private life insurance companies in terms of insurance policy, premium and commission during post-liberalisation period. It was observed from growth analysis that policy and premium collection of private companies was increasing significantly. Linear regression analysis showed high degree of correlation between policy and premium collection. Nena (2013) examined Indian life insurance industry for operating efficiency, growth of the LICI and importance of life insurance on human life. It was observed that the amount paid as way of claim had been increased each year. Results of F-test showed that variance of operating expense was highest and variance of investment was lowest. Insurers increased their business during post-reforms period. Quality of service and innovative product was expected to cover the uninsured population. Nagarajan, Ali and Sathyanarayana (2013) studied the Unit Linked Products of top five insurance companies in India. It was observed that PNB Met Life and Reliance Life performed better and market condition did not affect them. Kumari (2013) investigated the performance of Indian life insurance business during the post-liberalisation era. It was observed that CAGR of total life insurance premium was healthy. Total assets to premium income as well as investment income to total investment ratio were increasing year by year. Current ratio was more than one in Indian life insurance industry. Bawa and Chattha (2013) determined the impact of solvency, liquidity, leverage and size of life insurance companies on their performance. Linear regression analysis explained the significant positive relationship between return on assets and size of company and significant negative relationship between return on assets and capital of the company. Results of F-test verified the linear relationship among the variables. Chandrasekaran, Madhanagopal and Karthick (2013) investigated the company efficiency of life insurance sector for the year 2011. In this study, stochastic frontier analysis (SFA) provided insightful view of companies' level of efficiency and t-test measured that net investment income and net claims significantly contributed to total profit. Adigal and Mehta (2014) in their book edited changing financial system and economic perspective in India. The author analysed the savings mobilisation in Indian economy. Investment portfolio and financial institution were discussed. Jain (2014) analysed the difference between individual assurance and pension plan among the investments in the LICI. Individual assurance and pension plan had stable growth in initial three years and fluctuation in last two years. Results of t-test showed significant difference between premium collection and the insurance plan. Saha (2021) in his book elaborately discussed the status of life insurance and general insurance businesses of India with a special focus on regulatory framework in insurance industry.

1.4.3   Summary of Review of Literature

A brief summary of the above past studies is pointed out here:

(a) In some literature, savings mobilisation of life insurance companies in Indian financial market for development of economy is discussed. Investment in different sectors as per the IRDAI Regulations and investment policy during post-reforms period in this field are studied;

(b) During post-reforms period, traditional products and Unit Linked Products (ULIPs) as well as customer-oriented products have been incorporated;

(c) Influence of global markets on the growth, development and future prospect of Indian insurance industry are analysed;

(d) In past studies, reforms of life insurance sector in Indian life insurance industry have been recognised. Risk factors are not different in life insurance companies as public and private life insurance companies are regulated by the IRDAI.

1.4.4   Research Gap

Reviewing existing literature relating to the current study shows a research gap that leads to the objectives of present research work. Following are the important aspects of research gap:

(a) So far known, no in-depth study has been made to enquire an empirical study on insurance premium mobilisation and investment portfolio of the LICI and select other private life insurance companies in the post-reforms era;

(b) No study has been made, so far to explore the comparative development of the LICI and select private life insurance companies with regard to insurance premium mobilisation and investment portfolio during 2004–2005 to 2013–2014.

Against this background, the present study has been conducted with the following objectives.

1.5   OBJECTIVES OF THE STUDY

The major objectives of the study have been taken into consideration as follows:

(i) To review the historical evolution and regulatory framework of life insurance companies in India (*Refer to Chapter 2*);

(ii) To examine analytically insurance premium mobilisation and investment portfolio of the LICI and select private life insurance companies in the post-reforms era (*Refer to Chapter 3*);

(iii) To empirically assess the comparative relationships among the LICI and select private life insurance companies in terms of their insurance premium mobilisation and investment portfolio in the post-reforms era (*Refer to Chapter 4*);

(iv) To make a suitable conclusion of the study (*Refer to Chapter 5*).

1.6   RESEARCH METHODOLOGY

The present study is exploratory in nature. The methodology adopted in pursuing the study has been organised in the following paragraphs:

1.6.1   *Searching the Underlying Concept*

With a view to exploring the area under the study, an attempt has been made to study the available books, journals and annual reports on life insurance activities. These have been studied to acquire a general knowledge on the conceptual issues on life insurance activities, its problem areas and other issues. On the basis of theoretical knowledge, an effort has been made to chalk out the plan of work to make an empirical survey in order to empirically study insurance premium mobilisation and investment portfolio of the LICI and select private life insurance companies in India.

1.6.2   *Sample Design*

Totally, 24 life insurance companies, one public and 23 private life insurance companies, are operating in India. The study is being restricted to top seven life insurance companies (i.e. LICI and top six private life insurance companies). These top six private life insurance companies are selected out of 23 private life insurance companies using judgement sampling method on the basis of their total volume of the insurance premium mobilisation and investment portfolio during 2004–2005 to 2013–2014. Actually, two parameters—total insurance premium and total investments during the period 2004–2005 to 2013–2014—are considered separately to make two separate rankings of 23 private life insurance companies. Based on those two rankings, an average ranking of 23 private life insurance companies is made to select top six private life insurance companies out of them.

In order to validate such selection, an attempt has been made to find out: (a) the percentage of total life insurance premium collection of top six private life insurance companies to total premium collection of all 23 private life insurance companies and (b) the percentage of total investment of top six private life insurance companies to total investments of all 23 private life insurance companies during the study period of 2004–2005 to 2013–2014. While total volume of insurance premium mobilisation of 23 private life insurance companies is Rs. 573,547.69 crore, premium mobilisation of top six private life insurance companies is Rs. 408,044.38 crore during 2004–2005 to 2013–2014. The percentage of life insurance premium collection of top six private life insurance companies to total premium collection of 23 private life insurance companies is 71.14%. Moreover, total investment of 23 private life insurance companies is Rs. 1,807,512.34 crore, while total investment of six private life insurance companies is Rs. 1,341,182.24 crore during 2004–2005 to 2013–2014. The percentage of total investment of top six private life insurance companies to total investment of 23 private life insurance companies is 74.20%. Hence, method of selection of top six private life insurance companies as representative sample is quite appropriate. Selection of companies, collection of data and statistical tools are shown under the following heads.

1.6.3   Name of Select Life Insurance Companies

No	Life Insurance Company	
	Public Sector	Private Sector
1	Life Insurance Corporation of India (LICI)	-------
2	-------	ICICI – Prudential Life Insurance Company Ltd. (ICICI)
3	-------	Bajaj Allianz Life Insurance Company Ltd. (BAJAJ)
4	-------	SBI Life Insurance Company Ltd. (SBI)
5	-------	HDFC Standard Life Insurance Company Ltd. (HDFC)
6	-------	Birla Sun Life Insurance Company Ltd. (BIRLA)
7	-------	Max Life Insurance Company Ltd. (MAX)

1.6.4   Collection of Data

Chapter	Nature of Data	Source of Data
2	Secondary	Books, annual reports, journals, magazines, internet-based materials and online database of library
3 and 4	Secondary data collected during the pre-reforms period (2004–2005 to 2013–2014)	IRDAI, Annual Reports 2004–2005 to 2013–2014

1.6.5   Statistical Tools for Interpretation and Conclusion

Chapter	Nature of Analysis	Statistical Tools (if any)	Statistical Package (if any)
2	Conceptual Study	Nil	Nil
3	Empirical Study	• Year-Wise Growth Analysis • Log-linear Model • Pearson's Correlation Coefficient and t-test	SPSS 20.0
4		• One-Way ANOVA • Tukey's HSD Test • Independent sample t-test • Multiple Linear Regression Analysis (MLRA)	

1.7   LIMITATIONS OF THE STUDY

The study is subject to certain limitations as follows:

(i) The study is basically concerned with life insurance companies operating in India only;

(ii) This study does not cover any life insurance companies operating solely in other countries;

(iii) The study incorporates only available secondary data relating to insurance premium mobilisation and investment portfolio of the LICI and select private life insurance companies;

(iv) The study does not make financial performance analysis or efficiency analysis of life insurance companies;

(v) The study does not cover any comparative study between life insurance companies and general insurance companies.

1.8   THE SCHEME OF WORK

With a view to making an empirical study on premium mobilisation and investment portfolio of the LICI and select private life insurance companies in India, the study has been made through five chapters as follows:

- Chapter 1   Introduction *(Introducing the Theme; Research Problem; Research Questions, Review of Literature and Research Gap; Objectives of the Study; Research Methodology; Limitations of the Study and The Scheme of Work)*
- Chapter 2   Evolution and Regulatory Framework of Life Insurance Companies in India: A Conceptual Review
- Chapter 3   Premium Mobilization and Investment Portfolio by the LICI and Select Private Life Insurance Companies: An Analytical Study
- Chapter 4   An Empirical Insight into the Premium Mobilization and Investment Portfolio of the LICI and Select Private Life Insurance Companies in India
- Chapter 5   Concluding Observations and Suggestions

References

Adams, M., & Hardwick, P. (2003). Actuarial surplus management in United Kingdom Life Insurance Firms. *Journal of Business. Finance and Accounting*, 1–14.

Adigal, V. S., & Mehta, M. C. (2014). *Changing finance and economic perspectives*. Bharti Publications.

Balachandran, S. (2009). *Life insurance*. Insurance Institute of India.

Bawa, S. K., & Chattha, S. (2013). Financial performance of life insurance in Indian Insurance Industry. *Pacific Business Review International*, 1–9.

Bedi, H. S., & Singh, P. (2011). An empirical analysis of life insurance industry in India. *International Journal of Multidisciplinary Research*, 1–12.

Bhasin, N. (2007). *Banking and financial market in India 1947 to 2007*. Century Publication.

Bhole, L., & M. (2004). *Financial institutions and market*. TATA McGraw Hill Publishing Company Limited.

Chandra, S. C., & Ramesh, J. (2011). Lapsing of policies in life insurance sector-need for competitive strategies. *Journal on Banking Financial Services & Insurance Research*, 1–14.

Chandrasekaran, R., Madhanngopal R., & Kartik, K. (2013). A Stochastic Frontier Model on Investigating Efficiency of Life insurance Companies in India. *International Journal of Mathematics Trends and Technology*, 1–9

Das, B., & Mohanty, S. (2008). Mutual fund vs. life insurance: Behavioural analysis of retail investors. *International Journal of Business and Management*, 1–15.

Desai, V. (2005). *Financial system and development innovative success*. Himalaya Publishing House.

＃

Dickinson, G. (2011). Encouraging a dynamic life insurance industry: Economic benefits and policy issues. *City University Business School of London.*

Ege, I., & Bahadir, T. (2011). The relationship between insurance sector and economic growth: An econometric analysis. *IJER*, 1–12.

Gour, B., & Gupta, M. C. (2012). A review on solvency margin in Indian Insurance Companies. *International Journal of Recent Research and Review*, 1–5.

Gupta, A. (2003). *Insurance: A general text book.* Cyber Tech Publications.

Haridas, R. (2011). *Life insurance in India.* New Century Publication.

Henebry, K. L., & Diamond, J. (1998). Life insurance investment portfolio composition and investment regulations. *Journal of Insurance Issue*, 1–22.

Horton, J., & Macve, R. (1998). Planned changes in accounting principles for UK life insurance companies: A preliminary investigation of stock market impact. *Journal of Business Finance & Accounting*, 1–33.

IRDA, (Investment) (Amendment), Regulations, 2001.

IRDA, (Investment) (Amendment), Regulations, 2014.

Jain, R. (2014). Insurance: An investment opportunity & tool for risk management (A comparison between Individual Assurance and Pension Plans of LIC). *Pacific Business Review International* , 1–5.

Khan, M. Y. (2006). *Indian financial system.* Tata McGraw Hill Publishing Company Limited.

Koijen, R. S. J., & Yogo, M. (2013). The cost of financial frictions for life insurers. *SSRN.COM/abstract=2031993*, 1–50.

Kumar, D. (1991). *Tryst with trust: The LIC story.* LIC of India.

Kumar, V., & Kumari, P. (2012). A comparative study on public vs private sector in life insurance. *VSRD International Journal of Business and Management Research*, 1–3.

Kumari, T. H. (2013). Performance evaluation of Indian Life Insurance Industry in post liberalization. *International Journal of Social Sciences Arts and Humanities*, 1–8.

Lee, C. C., Lee, C. C., & Chiu, Y. B. (2013). *The link between life insurance activities and economic growth: Some new evidence*, 1–23.

Mahdzan, N. S., & Victorian, S. M. P. (2013). Determinants of life insurance demand: A focus on saving motives and financial literacy. *Canadian Centre of Science and Education*, 1–11.

Nagarajan, G., Asif, A., & Sathyanarayana, N. (2013). A study on performance of Unit-Linked Insurance Plans (ULIP Offered by Indian Private Insurance Companies. *International Journal of Advanced Research in Management and Social Sciences* , 1–14.

Negi, D., & Singh, P. (2012). Demographic analysis of factors influencing purchase of life insurance products in India. *European Journal of Business and Management*, 1–13.

Nena, S. (2013). Performance evaluation of Life Insurance Corporation (LIC) of India. *International Journal of Advance Research in Computer Science and Management Studies*, 1–6.

Niwata, N. (1971). The economic theory of insurance and social security, 37–68.

Noronh, M. R. (2012). A comparative study of cost efficiency of life insurance companies in India. *GFJMR*, 1–14.

Padhi, B. (2013). Role & performances of private insurance companies in India, in the post liberalization era. *International Journal of Engineering, Business and Enterprise Applications*, 1–7.

Palande, P. S. Shah, R. S., & Lunawat, M. L. (2003). *Insurance India changing policies and emerging opportunities*. Response Books.

Panda, B. N., & Panda, J. K. (2012). A factorial analysis of mutual fund investment and insurance fund investment: A comparative study. *Journal of Business Management, Commerce & Research*, 1–11.

Pathak, B. V. (2006). *The Indian financial system*. Pearson Education.

Plantin, G., & Rochet, J. C. (2007). *When insurers go bust–an economic analysis of the role and design of prudential regulations*. Princeton University Press.

Rai, A., & Medha, S. (2013). The antecedents of customer loyalty: An empirical investigation in life insurance context. *Journal of Competitiveness*, 1–25.

Rajendran, R., & Natarajan, B. (2009). The impact of LPG on Life Insurance Corporation of India (LIC). *Asia Pacific Journal of Finance and Banking Research*, 1–12.

Saad, N. M., & Idris, N. E. H. (2011). Efficiency life insurance company in Malaysia and Brunei: A comparative study. *International Journal of Humanities and Social Science*, 1–12.

Saha, S. S. (2013). *Indian financial system and markets*. Tata McGraw Hill Education Private Limited.

Saha, S. S. (2021). *Indian financial system: Financial markets, institutions and services* (2nd ed.). Tata McGraw Hill.

Satpathy, S., & Sahoo, R. (2012). Effectiveness of executives–A Comparison between different insurance sectors. *VSRD International Journal of Business & Management Research*, 1–6.

Skipper, H. D., & Jean, K. W. (2007). *Risk management and insurance perspectives in a global economy*. Blackwell Publishing.

Upadhyay, Y., & Shrivastawa, R. K. (2007). *Risk management in banking and insurance*. Deep & Deep Publication Private Limited.

CHAPTER 2

Evolution and Regulatory Framework of Life Insurance Companies in India: A Conceptual Review

Abstract The main objective of this chapter is to conceptually review (a) the evolution of the life insurance industry in different parts of the world and India especially in the pre- and post-independence era; (b) current structure of life insurance industry operating in India; and (c) regulatory framework governing life insurance business in the pre- and post-independence era with special emphasis on regulatory framework governing portfolio investments of life insurance companies. Before independence, Indian life insurance industry was dominated by mainly British life insurance companies and the applicable regulations were made keeping in view their interest. After India's independence, nationalisation of the LICI by bringing together numerous small insurance companies was a significant event in India's life insurance history. After financial sector reforms, private participation, technology up-gradation, numerous products and after sale service have enhanced the efficiency of the life insurance sector. The entire life insurance sector was brought under the ambit of the IRDAI. The IRDAI has also regulated the total fund of the life insurance companies into three segments, like life fund, pension and annuity fund, and ULIP fund. In the pre-reform era, investments were made in Government and approved securities, while it has been extended to infrastructure and social sectors in the post-reform era.

© The Author(s), under exclusive license to Springer Nature
Singapore Pte Ltd. 2022
S. P. Patra et al., *Investment Pattern of LICI and Select Private LICs
in the Post-reforms Era in India*,
https://doi.org/10.1007/978-981-19-2799-7_2

Keywords Evolution of LICs · Overview of life insurance sector · Regulatory framework · IRDAI · Insurance sector reforms

2.1   INTRODUCTION

The previous chapter, the introductory one, provides a brief idea of the theme of the research, statement of the research problem, a sketch on review of the literature, objectives of the study, research methodology, limitations of the study and a scheme of work. The evolution of the life insurance industry, an overview of life insurance industry currently operational in India and regulatory framework governing life insurance business have been studied in the current chapter. The evolution of life insurance business in different parts of the world including India is discussed in detail. Evolution in India has been discussed by segmenting it into pre- and post-independence period. Post-independence period has again been segmented into pre- and post-reforms period. On the other hand, regulatory framework governing life insurance industry has also been discussed by segmenting it into pre- and post-independence period. Regulatory framework governing portfolio investments of life insurance companies has also been discussed with special emphasis.

2.2   EVOLUTION OF LIFE INSURANCE INDUSTRY

2.2.1   World Scenario

The concept of insurance had been used almost 4500 years ago by the Babylonians, the Greeks and the Romans, but in modern sense, it was originated in the Mediterranean during thirteenth or fourteenth centuries (Saha, 2021). Insurance as organised activity came into force at different times at different stages in different countries. Marine insurance is the oldest type of insurance and European nautical nations made first insurance contracts in 1347 (Pathak, 2006). Eight insurance contracts were drawn in Genoa by a notary in 1393. In England, Lombard merchants brought marine insurance from Italy. This was followed by life insurance business. Hence, life insurance came to light on the basis of the marine insurance. Marine insurance underwriters were the first life assurers. They issued policies on the life of merchants, master and the crews of the ship sailing on the sea along with the goods. If ship was captured, the insurer paid the amount needed to release the captain and its sailors. The contracts were made for temporary assurance by private individuals (underwriters) for a short period during the reign of the Queen Elizabeth. First recorded life insurance policy was issued on the life of the William Gibbons for 12 months at the rate of 8% on 18 June 1583 AD in England and 16 underwriters were responsible to bear the risk of this policy. In eighteenth century, some important life assurance societies were the Amicable Society (1705). Initially, the amount payable on death by the society was fluctuating. However, since 1757, they started paying a fixed amount on death. The Equitable Life Assurance Society (1762) used Mortality Table in calculating sum assured on death (Trivedi, 2008). The Westminster Society (1792) and Old Equitable, England (1756), are some of the life insurers at that time. Premium was charged on the basis of reputation and condition of the health of the insured. Speculations were also made on the amount of premium to be payable on an insurance policy. In 1774, Life Assurance Act (also known as Gambling Act) was passed to end the speculation in life insurance business. In the nineteenth century, a large number of life insurance companies were formed. Many of them failed to continue and some merged their operation with others. At that time, the Life Insurance Act, 1870 and its subsequent amendment, the Life Insurance Act, 1871, were passed to control the life insurance business properly. The Assurance Companies Act issued in 1909 had replaced all the previous acts and was applied to all classes of insurance businesses. Later on, various acts were passed such as Industrial Assurance Act, 1923, Assurance Companies Act, 1946, Insurance Companies Act, 1958, and the Companies Act, 1967 (Sharma, 2010).

India had preserved the traces of insurance in the ancient Indian history in the form of marine trade loan. Insurance in India had deep-rooted history in the Hindu mythology, especially in the Vedas (Pathak, 2006). In Rig-Veda, it was observed that the Aryans had derived a system of communal insurance nearly 3000 years ago (in 1000 BC) known as Yogakshema (meaning well-being) as a measure of protection against the devastation in future. It was mentioned in the writings of Manu (Manusmriti), the Yagnavalkya (Dharmasastra) and Kautilya (Arthasastra) (Saha, 2021). These writings talked about pooling of resources for redistribution in the times of natural calamities. The Vedic Rishis also knew this concept. Joint family system and their mutual help in the Aryan society developed a self-insurance system as an important part of social cooperation. The Hindu Society of India, during this time, practised this principle. This social structure was mentioned in the Manusmriti and the Arthasastra. Social codes were designed to provide security to all in the community. Thus, the concept of insurance, which was found in the Rig-Veda and the Upanishads, was known to the Hindus. They also used marine insurance in the overseas trades (Gopalakrishana, 2010).

2.2.2   *Indian Scenario*

2.2.2.1   *Pre-independence Era*

Before the British rule, some informal insurance system was found in India. However, life insurance in modern form was brought to India from the England, when the British companies started the life insurance business and started issuing life policies for European civilian and soldiers. The Bombay Insurance Company Ltd. was the first life insurance company founded in 1793 for insuring the lives of only the British people in India. In 1818, the British formed an English life insurance company named the Oriental Life Insurance Company in Calcutta. It was operational till 1934. This was followed by the establishment of the Bombay Life Assurance Company in 1823 in Bombay and the Madras Equitable Life Insurance Society in 1829 at Madras Presidency. All of these life insurance companies did not issue life policies to people of Indian origin till 1870. Later, these companies started issuing life policies to Indians against payment of extra premium. This unbiased system spread the nationalistic and patriotic ideas to form Indian life insurance companies. As a result, the Bombay Mutual Life Assurance Society Ltd. was formed on 3 December 1870, which was the first Indian life insurance company to sell the policies to the Indians at normal rate. First balance sheet of life insurance business was prepared in July 1871. Some other notable Indian companies involved in the business were Oriental Government Security Life Assurance Company Ltd. (1874), the Bharat Insurance Company (1896) at Bombay Residency and the Empire of India Life Insurance Company Ltd. (1897) (Trivedi, 2008).

After the failure of a number of insurance companies, the British Insurance Act, 1870, was enacted by the British Government and the act was in force for three decades (Pathak, 2006). During this tenure, foreign companies enjoyed monopoly in life insurance business. Major foreign companies during this tenure were Albert Life Insurance, Royal Insurance, Liverpool and London Global Insurance (History of Insurance, www.irdai.gov.in). At that time, it was difficult to sell assurance contracts to people outside presidency towns. The next most important life insurance company, Oriental Government Security Life Assurance Company, was established on 5 May 1874. This company brought the life insurance within the reach of Indians with modest income group. Large number of Indian insurance companies was formed under the Indian Companies Act, 1866. Oriental Government Security Life Assurance Company was the leader among the Indian insurance companies (Kumar, 1991). The Bharat Insurance Company was launched by Lala Harikishan Lal in 1896 at Lahore in erstwhile Punjab. This was followed by the Empire of India Life Insurance Company Ltd. founded by Ernest Fedrik Allum and Rustomji Bharucha in 1897 at the advent of twentieth century. It was set up as movement to the boycott of the British institutions because by then Indians realised the potential of Indian insurance business.

The Swadeshi Movement of 1905–1907 created more insurance companies. United India in Madras and National Indian and Co-operative Assurance at Lahore were established in 1906. Hindustan Co-operative Insurance Company in Calcutta (1907) and the Swadeshi Life in Bombay (1908) were formed subsequently. Thereafter, various other insurance companies, like New India, Jupiter and Lakshmi, were formed as a result of Swadeshi Movement of 1905. However, there was no specific Insurance Act for life insurance business until 1912. The Swadeshi Movement of 1905, the Non-cooperation Movement of 1919 and the Civil Disobedience Movement of 1929 opened up new opportunities to the younger generation for constructive national services. This sprit boosted the insurance activity, and a need to regulate the insurance companies was felt. As a result, Life Insurance Companies Act, 1912, Provident Insurance Societies Act, 1912, and Indian Life Insurance Act, 1912, were passed by the Government of India on the basis of the model of the British Insurance Act, 1909 (Trivedi, 2008). These acts were introduced to stop discrimination between Indian companies and foreign companies working in India. All Indian Life Assurance Offices Association (AILAOA) was formed in 1927 to protect the interest of Indian companies. The leaders of national movement created a pressure to stop this discrimination. Then, the Government of India decided to pass a stop-gap act by amending the Life Insurance Companies Act, 1912. In 1928, the Indian Insurance Companies Act was enacted to collect the statistical information about life insurance business (Sharma, 2010). The AILAOA created pressure upon the Government to enact a separate insurance act in 1932, with regard to registration of life insurance companies. In response to this, the Government appointed Mr. S. C. Sen, a solicitor and an officer on special duty, to study and report on the amendment of the Insurance Act. In 1936, the AILAOA formed an informal committee and submitted their report on this amendment. Finally, the chairman, Sir N. N. Sarcar, and the then law member of the informal committee examined the report of Mr. S. C. Sen for amendment of the Insurance Act in India. Based on their recommendations, Provident Insurance Societies Act, 1912, and Indian Life Insurance Act, 1912, were consolidated and amended by the Insurance Act, 1938, for regulating investment of insurance fund, income and expenditure, and management of insurance companies. Following this amendment, all Indian and foreign life insurance businesses working in India were brought under a unified control. Several amendments to the act were made in 1939, 1940, 1944 and 1945 to address the shortcomings in matter of licensing of agent, maintenance of account, expenses on commission and investment of fund of insurance companies (Kumar, 1991). It helped almost uninterrupted growth in life insurance business during this period.

2.2.2.2   Post-independence Era

On 15 August 1947, India got its freedom, which made it difficult for foreign life insurance businesses to compete with the Indian life insurance businesses. Out of 105 foreign insurance companies, only 15 life insurance companies operated successfully in 1955. Despite the record progress made by Indian life insurance companies after independence, life insurance business was only an urban phenomenon. During this time, both public and policyholders lost the confidence on life insurance businesses for their malpractices and resultant liquidation. Agencies entrusted with the responsibility of controlling these companies aided these malpractices. The Government of India did not make any specific investment policy initially. So, the large financiers controlling the life insurance businesses used the funds to serve their own purpose or for speculative purposes, even in their own other enterprises using the loopholes of insurance act. Hence, the fund got interlocked in banking and insurance businesses only. This system harmed the interest of the policyholders and growth of the life insurance business. These increased the malpractice in the insurance sector (Kumar, 1991). An investment policy was felt necessary to remove the malpractice in the investment of life funds. In April 1945, Cowasji Jehangir Committee was constituted by the Indian Government to check manipulation and interlocking of funds between banks and insurance companies. Consequently, the Insurance Act, 1950, was passed by the Indian Parliament on the committee's recommendation. The act authorised the Controller of Insurance into inspection of the financial books, rectification of investment proportion of the life fund in the Government securities and approved securities. It controlled manipulation of funds to the some extent (Palande et al., 2003). However, the Government's effort to regulate the life insurance businesses through various insurance acts was not very effective. The process of winding up of insurance companies was also totally unknown to the Government. So, the state control was necessary. Hence, the Government of India opted for nationalisation of life insurance industry to avoid malpractices; protect interest of the policyholders; control long-term insurance fund; and use life fund for social and economic development. All India National Congress (AINC), a political party in India, included the concept of nationalisation of life insurance business in its manifesto at Avadi Session of the Parliament in 1955. In this view, all the political parties in India resolved that the life insurance business should be nationalised. On 19 January 1956, management of the 245 Indian and foreign insurers and provident societies operating in India was taken over by the Indian Government through Life Insurance Ordinance, 1956. This ordinance was replaced by Life Insurance (Emergency) Provisions Act, 1956. The bill was introduced in the parliament in February 1956, and it became an act in July 1956. Ultimately, life insurance business was nationalised on 1 September 1956 by the signature of the President of India. So, all the life insurance companies were brought under one umbrella and LICI was formed. Sri Kamat joined as the deputy chairman of the LICI on 1 February 1957 and became the chairman of the LICI on 5 June 1957. In May 1957, the LICI introduced the Janata Policy Scheme to cover the needs of insurance industry and rural working population. In the 1957, the Government introduced a bill in the parliament to make an investment board. However, at that time, the Mundhra episode was being enquired by Justice Chagla and the bill was dropped. Similar suggestion was also made by first estimate committee report (1960–1961), but it was also turned down. The detailed investment policy was adopted in 1958 after the Mundhra scandal to provide maximum safety and security to the policyholder's funds and maximise the rate of return on the investment. Portfolio of investment had changed from time to time based on national priorities and emerging market conditions subject to the statutory limit (Khan, 2006). However, the policy always maintained certain principles, such as dispersion over different industries, regions and sectors; economic and social development; safety and security of shareholders of funds; avoidance of speculation; maximisation of return on investment; care in case of investment in shares or debentures; and avoidance of conflict of interest (Kumar, 1991). On 1 July 1958, the investment policy of the LICI was considered. In September 1958, the executive committee took a stand to declare the bonus on the basis of capacity of the insurers rather than the way bonuses were paid in the past by the insurers. The Government of India made an administrative reforms commission (ARC) on 5 January 1966 under the chairmanship of Shri Mararji Desai, and the report was submitted on 7 October 1968. After this commission, the Mararka Committee was appointed by the Government on 21 July 1967 to enquire the high level of expenses of the LICI and the committee submitted the report on 30 April 1969. Another important decision by the Government in 1970 was to form an informal group under the chairmanship of Shri S. Jagannathan to look into the portfolio of investment and the investment policy of the LICI. This group submitted the report in December 1971. Then, the Nayudu Committee was formed on 31 August 1971 under the chairmanship of Shri N. V. Nayudu and this committee submitted their report on 3 November 1971 with some recommendations with regard to the functions of zonal offices of LICI (Palande et al., 2003). The Thaper Committee was made to examine the recommendation of the Nayudu Committee in December 1974, and as per its recommendation, the Government revised its earlier decision to abolish zonal offices and allowed them to continue with limited functions. In October 1977, the Ramanathan Committee recommended that the zonal offices should continue their operations. In January 1979, the committee of actuaries was constituted to examine the premium rate and its possible revision. Based on the recommendation of the committee, the LICI decided to revise the premium rate under various plans of assurance with effect from 1 April 1980. On 18 May 1979, the Era Sezhiyan Committee was formed under the chairmanship of Mr. Era Sezhiyan to review the working of the LICI. The committee submitted its report on 30 September 1980 with regard to the development of life insurance businesses, service to policyholder, expenses of management, investment of assets, management of human resource, organisational structure, etc. The committee recommended splitting up the LICI into five non-competing corporations to provide more effective realisation of the objectives of nationalisation. The bill containing the matter was introduced in the parliament on 19 December 1983. However, it lapsed in December 1984. The LICI extended its business in other countries since June 1992.

2.2.2.3 Pre-reforms Era

In the pre-reforms scenario, foreign life insurers dominated the life insurance business in India. Statutory measures to control the life insurance business were weak, and level of competition among the existing foreign insurers was high till the end of nineteenth century. From the beginning of twentieth century, a large number of Indian life insurance companies entered the market. There were many allegations of unfair trade practices in the life insurance business. On the top of that, the Insurance Act discriminated between the Indian and foreign life insurance companies. Frauds and malpractices in the usage of life fund persisted even after the introduction of the Insurance Act, 1938. In 1956, the Government of India merged the private life insurance companies and provident fund societies into Life Insurance Corporation of India (LICI). Since then, the LICI enjoyed complete monopoly in the life insurance business in India. During this tenure, there was a lack of awareness about life insurance products.

2.2.2.4 Post-reforms Era

In the post-reforms era, the Insurance Regulatory and Development Authority (IRDA) ended the monopoly of LICI, the only public limited company in Indian life insurance sector, and opened it up for private life insurance players with Indian or indo-foreign ownership. They increased the life insurance penetration and competition in the market. It forced the LICI and other private life insurers to offer a wider choice of life insurance products to the customer from rural and urban population at lower price, better customer service, superior information technology and higher return on the investment of the life insurance fund through an investment portfolio controlled and monitored by the IRDA. The Indian economy has been benefited by the performance of the life insurance business. At present, 24 life insurance companies are operating in India.

2.3   OVERVIEW OF LIFE INSURANCE COMPANIES OPERATING IN INDIA

In this segment, a brief overview of 24 life insurers currently operating in India is made. These 24 companies are comprised of one public life insurance company (LICI) and 23 private life insurance companies. The product approval committee approves the product of the life insurance companies. This committee examines the viability of the products, which were submitted before it by the insurers. Main aim of the IRDAI was to ensure transparency in terms of benefit payouts, which may allow the customers to choose the right policy in accordance with their needs. Number of life insurance products and office of these 24 companies during the year 2013–2014 are shown here (overview of 24 life insurers, available at: shodganga.inflibnet.ac.in) (Table 2.1).

The brief overview of 24 life insurers (Sinha & Gandhi, 2014) as on 2014 is depicted in Table 2.2.

2.4   REGULATORY FRAMEWORK GOVERNING LIFE INSURANCE BUSINESS

The life insurance business is one of the most important businesses in the world. It requires well-defined regulatory system. Regulator should confirm that the companies are performing under its supervision and protects the policyholders against the malpractice of life insurance business and implements it in a manner so that growth of the industry is not hampered. Regulatory framework of Indian life insurance industry has always been very comprehensive.

While investment of life fund in Indian financial market was a significant issue, initially the Government of India did not make any specific policy for this purpose. Hence, shareholders controlling the life insurance companies used life funds to serve their own interests. That was harmful for the interests of the policyholders and growth of the life insurance business. It increased misuse of the fund. Insurance Act and other regulations were amended to serve the vested interest of the shareholders (Kumar, 1991). Regulations governing Indian insurance business in the pre- and post-independence era are discussed here.

Table 2.1 Products and offices of Indian life insurers

No.	Name of insurer	Number of product (non-linked and linked)	Micro-product		Number of office
			Individual category	Group category	
Public Sector					
1	Life Insurance Corporation of India (LICI)	20	01	–	4839
Private Sector					
2	Aegon Religare	24	–	–	93
3	Aviva Life	31	–	–	121
4	Bajaj Alliance	18	–	–	759
5	Bharti AXA	18	–	01	123
6	Birla Sun Life	32	04	01	123
7	Canara HSBC OBC	16	–	01	32
8	DLF Pramerica	14	–	–	61
9	Exide Life	19	–	–	201
10	Edelweiss Tokio	38	02		60
11	Future Generali	23	–	–	98
12	HDFC Standard	36	01	–	429
13	ICICI Prudential	20	02	–	557
14	IDBI Federal	08	–	01	62
15	India First	15	–	–	48
16	Kotak Mahindra	35	–	–	206
17	Max Life	20	–	–	287
18	PNB MetLife	18	01	–	161
19	Reliance Life	31	–	–	911
20	Sahara India	07	01	–	142
21	SBI Life	24	01	02	762
22	Shriram Life	16	–	02	263
23	Star Union Dai-ichi	10	–	–	69
24	TATA AIA	11	–	–	170
Total		504	13	08	10,577

Source IRDAI Annual Report 2013–2014

2.4.1 *Regulatory Framework in the Pre-independence Era*

Life insurance helps a person to bear the risk in the future for his family arising out of his untimely death. With a view to creating public trust and ensuring social justice, regulations in the life insurance business

Table 2.2 Brief overview of life insurance companies

Sl. No.	Life insurer	Salient points
1	Aegon Religare Life Insurance Company Ltd. (Aegon Religare Life Insurance Company, About Company available at: http://www.aegonreligare.com)	• Founded in collaboration of Aegon, one of the leading life insurance companies in India, Religare, leading integrated financial services groups in India and Bennett, Coleman & Co., largest media house in India • Performs policy servicing on the phone via Interactive Voice Response System (IVR) by issuing the customer with T-Pin for authentication • Includes first time medical report of customer in the policy kit • Launched a suite of product that is focussed on providing the customer to meet their long-term financial goal • Capital contribution by promoters of Indian and foreign origin is more than Rs. 950 crore and Rs. 300 crore, respectively
2	Aviva Life Insurance Company Ltd. (Aviva Life Insurance Company, Company Profile available at: http://www.avivaindia.com)	• Joint venture between the Dabur Invest Corp (DIC) and the Aviva International Holdings Limited (AIH), an UK-based insurance group • Current capital is more than Rs. 2000 crore • Shareholding: DIC 74% and AIH 26% • Customers across 16 countries • Introduced many innovative sales approaches • Introduced the contemporary Unit Linked Product (ULIP)
3	Bajaj Allianz Life Insurance Company Ltd. (Bajaj Allianz Life Insurance Company, About Company available at: http://www.bajajallianz.com)	• Joint venture between the Allianz SE and the Bajaj Finserv Ltd. • Reputation of high technical expertise • Comprehensive and innovative solution for customer • In-depth market knowledge and goodwill of 'Bajaj' brand • Strong portfolio of the different life insurance products • Capital contribution by promoters of Indian and foreign origin is more than Rs. 100 crore and Rs. 30 crore, respectively

Sl. No.	Life insurer	Salient points
4	Bharti AXA Life Insurance Company Ltd. (Bharti AXA Life Insurance Company, About Company available at: https://www.bharti-axalife.com)	• Founded in collaboration of Bharti Enterprises (a pioneering force in the telecom sector with over 110 million customers) and the AXA (operating in Western Europe, North America, and Asia/Pacific Region, Australia, New Zealand, Hong Kong, Singapore, Indonesia, Philippines, Thailand, China, India and Malaysia) • Shareholding: The Bharti holds 74% stake and the AXA holds the rest 26% • Capital contribution by promoters of Indian and foreign origin is more than Rs. 1500 crore and Rs. 400 crore, respectively • Started its operations in India in December 2006 • Products are primary focussed on wealth management
5	Birla Sun Life Insurance Company Ltd. (Birla Sun Life Insurance Company, Company Profile, available at: http://insurance.birlasunlife.com)	• Established in 2001 • Joint venture between the Aditya Birla Group, an Indian multinational conglomerate with presence in India, Thailand, Indonesia, Malaysia, Philippines, Egypt, Canada, Australia and China, and the Sun Life Financial in Canada • Capital contribution by promoters of Indian and foreign origin is more than Rs. 1400 crore and Rs. 450 crore, respectively • Introduced 'Free Look Period' for the first time and the same was made mandatory by the IRDAI for all other life insurance companies • Pioneered to launch of ULIPs among private players
6	Canara HSBC Life OBC Life Insurance Company Ltd. (Sinha & Gandhi, 2014)	• Joint venture of Canara Bank holding 51% equity, HSBC Insurance (Asia Pacific) Ltd. holding 26% equity and Oriental Bank of Commerce holding 23% equity • Capital contribution by promoters of Indian and foreign origin is more than Rs. 700 crore and Rs. 240 crore, respectively • Commenced business on 16 June 2008 • Access to above 60 million customers through a pan-India network of around 7000 branches of Canara bank

(continued)

Table 2.2 (continued)

Sl. No.	Life insurer	Salient points
7	DHFL Pramerica Life Insurance Company Ltd. (DHFL Pramerica Life Insurance Company, Company Details available at: https://www.dhflpramerica.com)	• Joint venture of DLF Limited and Prudential Financial Inc. (PFI), USA which also offered the trade name, 'Pramerica' • Wide range of life insurance solution for individual as well as group • Capital contribution by promoters of Indian and foreign origin is more than Rs. 250 crore and Rs. 80 crore, respectively
8	Edelweiss Tokio Life Insurance Company Ltd. (Edelweiss Tokio Life Insurance Company, Company Profile available at: http://www.edelweisstokio.in)	• Joint venture between Edelweiss Financial Services (Mumbai), a leading diversified financial service group in India, and Tokio Marine Holdings Inc. (Japan), oldest (130 years) and largest insurance player in Japan having operational base in 39 countries • Capital contribution by promoters of Indian and foreign origin is more than Rs. 130 crore and Rs. 40 crore, respectively
9	Exide Life Insurance Company Ltd. (Exide Life Insurance Company, About Company available at: http://www.exidelife.in)	• Formerly ING Vysya Life Insurance Company Ltd • Started its operations in 2001 with head quarter in Bangalore • Serves over 10 lakh customers across the India and manages over Rs. 8,800 crore in assets • Fully owned by Exide Industries Limited • Equity capital is Rs.1600 crore • Channels of distribution include over 35,000 advisors and huge customer care centres across the country • Distribution relationships with bank, corporate agent and broker, and referral partner

Sl. No.	Life insurer	Salient points
10	Future Generali India Life Insurance Company Ltd. (Future Generali India Life Insurance Company, General Views available at: http://www.futuregenerali.in)	• Joint venture between the Italy-based Generali Group and the India-based Future Group • Incorporated in September 2007 • Issued over 11 lakh policies • Provides a complete range of simplified solutions for the financial security of individual and group • Issues ULIP • Capital contribution by promoters of Indian and foreign origin is more than Rs. 1000 crore and Rs. 350 crore, respectively
11	HDFC Standard Life Insurance Company Ltd. (HDFC Standard Life Insurance Company Ltd., About History, available at: http://www.hdfclife.com)	• One of the most important private life insurers in India • Provides individual and group insurance solution to customers • Life insurance products: term, endowment and pension • Joint venture between the HDFC Ltd. largest housing finance institution in India and the Standard Life Plc., leading financial service provider in the UK • First private life insurer that got registered by the IRDAI on 23 October 2000 • Shareholding: The HDFC (70.64%); Standard Life (26%); other companies (rest) • Capital contribution by promoters of Indian and foreign origin is more than Rs. 1400 crore and Rs. 500 crore, respectively • High-quality financial consultancy • Over 400 branches and service centres over 900 cities and towns in India Various customer-centric product solutions for life protection, pension, savings and investment for women and children

(continued)

Table 2.2 (continued)

Sl. No.	Life insurer	Salient points
12	ICICI Prudential Life Insurance Company Ltd. (ICICI Prudential Life Insurance Company, Company Profile available at: http://www.iciciprulife.com)	• Joint venture between the ICICI Bank Ltd., a leading private sector bank in India, and the Prudential Plc, a leading international financial services group in the UK • Shareholding: ICICI Bank (74%) and Prudential Plc (26%) • Capital contribution by promoters of Indian and foreign origin is more than Rs. 1000 crore and Rs. 350 crore, respectively • Started operations on 24 November 2000 • Asset under management (AUM) is more than Rs. 800 billion
13	IDBI Federal Life Insurance Company Ltd. (IDBI Federal Life Insurance Company, Company Profile available at: http://www.idbifederal.com)	• Joint venture among three leading financial conglomerates: (a) IDBI Bank Ltd., a leading private sector bank in India; (b) Federal Bank Ltd.; and (c) Ageas, a multinational insurance giant in Europe • Launched its operation in March 2008 • Nationwide network of customers of IDBI Bank, Federal Bank and a sizeable network of advisors and partner • Sum assured of all the products issued so far is more than Rs. 40,000 crores • Foreign and Indian equity capital in the total capital is more than Rs. 200 crores and Rs. 500 crores, respectively
14	IndiaFirst Life Insurance Company Ltd. (IndiaFirst life Insurance Company, Company Profile available at: http://www.indiafirstlife.com)	• Youngest company in India • Founded in collaboration of Bank of Baroda, Andhra Bank and Legal and General (UK) with a capital base of Rs. 455 crore • One of the most capital competent life insurance companies in the industry • Shareholding: BoB (44%); Andhra Bank (30%); and Legal and General (26%) • Capital contribution by promoters of foreign and Indian origin is more than Rs. 100 crores and Rs. 350 crores, respectively

Sl. No.	Life insurer	Salient points
15	Kotak Mahindra Old Mutual Life Insurance Company Ltd. (Kotak Mahindra, About History available at http://insurance.kotak.com)	• Joint venture between Kotak Mahindra Bank Ltd. (KMBL) and Old Mutual Life Insurance • One of the leading financial institutions in India and offers a range of financial service in different sectors • Indian and foreign promoters hold more than Rs. 350 crores and Rs. 130 crores, respectively, in the company • Started its operation on 10 January 2000 • Shareholding: KMBL (74%) and Old Mutual (26%)
16	Life Insurance Corporation of India (LICI) (Dominant Role, LICI, available at https://www.shodganga.inflibnet.ac.in)	• One of the fastest growing life insurance companies in India • Only public sector company • Autonomous body incorporated as per the provisions of the LIC Act passed in the parliament on 19 June 1956 • Date of formation: 1 September 1956 • Distribute life insurance products much more broadly particular to the rural areas with a view to reach all potential insurable persons in this country and to provide people in India sufficient financial cover at a rational cost as well as to use resources for economic development of India • Dominant market share even after 19 years of reforms
17	Max Life Insurance Company Ltd. (Max Life Insurance Company Ltd. About History available at: http://www.maxlifeinsurance.com)	• Joint venture between Max India Ltd., a multi-business corporation in India, and Mitsui Sumitomo Company Ltd., member of MS&AD insurance group, top general insurance group in Japan • Indian and foreign promoter holds more than Rs. 1400 crores and Rs. 500 crores, respectively, in the company • Provides diversified life insurance products for long-term savings and life protection • High-quality customer service and customer-centric operation • Possess financial stability and investment expertise

(continued)

Table 2.2 (continued)

Sl. No.	Life insurer	Salient points
18	PNB MetLife India Insurance Company Ltd. (PNB MetLife India Insurance Company, About PNB available at: http://www.pnbmetlife.com)	• Formerly MetLife India Insurance Company Ltd. (MetLife India) • Joint venture among MetLife International Holdings Inc. (MIHI), Punjab National Bank Limited (PNB), Jammu & Kashmir Bank Limited (JKB), M. Pallonji and Company Private Ltd. and other private investors • MIHI and PNB are the majority shareholders • Capital contributions by promoters of foreign and Indian origin are more than Rs. 500 crores and Rs. 1400 crores, respectively • Provides a wide range of life insurance products through its 10,000 financial advisors and multiple bank partners • Provides access to the employee benefit plans for over 800 corporate clients in India
19	Reliance Nippon Life Insurance Company Ltd. (Reliance Life Insurance Company, Company Profile available at: http://www.reliancelife.com)	• Profit-making company for the last four financial years • One of the top private life insurers • Segment of Reliance Capital, one of the top private sector NBFC having business in asset management, mutual fund, stock broking, life and general insurance, proprietary investment, private equity and other activities in financial services • The Nippon Life Insurance Company (also known as Nissay), Japan's largest private life insurer acquired 26% of its stake • Foreign and Indian equity capital in the company is more than Rs. 300 crores and Rs. 850 crores, respectively

Sl. No.	Life insurer	Salient points
20	Sahara India Life Insurance Company Ltd. (Shodhganga, Chapter, available at: http://shodhganga.inflibnet.ac.in)	• Venture of the Sahara Pariwar, the world's largest 'family-based business' with diversified business interests • Granted license on 6 February 2004 • First wholly Indian private life insurance company • Initial capital Rs. 157 crore • Currently, total capital is more than Rs. 2000 crores • Offers both individual and group insurance products
21	SBI Life Insurance Company Ltd. (SBI Life Insurance Company, Content available at: http://www.sbilife.co.in)	• Collaboration between State Bank of India (SBI), the leading banking franchise in India, and the Cardif of France • Shareholding: SBI (74%); Cardif (26%) • Authorised capital is Rs. 2000 crore • Foreign and Indian partners hold Rs. 260 crore and Rs.740 crore, respectively • Has a unique multi-distribution channel and uses the SBI Group as a platform for life insurance products
22	Shriram Life Insurance Company Ltd. (Shriram Life Insurance Company, Profile available at: http://www.shriramlife.com)	• Joint venture between the Chennai-based Shriram Group, one of the largest and well-managed financial service conglomerates in India, and the Suid-Africaanse Nasionale Lewens Assuransie Maatskappij Beperk (SANLAM) (also known as South African National Life Assurance Company Ltd.), one of the largest life insurance and asset management firms in South Africa • Launched its operation in India in December 2005 • Indian equity capital is Rs.175 crore • Significantly focussed on inclusive growth of the rural customers

(continued)

Table 2.2 (continued)

Sl. No.	Life insurer	Salient points
23	Star Union Dai-ichi Life Insurance Company Ltd. (Star Union Dai-ichi Life Insurance Company, About Company available at: https://www.sudlife.in)	• Joint venture of the Bank of India (BOI) and the Union Bank of India, two leading public sector banks in India and the Dai-ichi (Number One) Mutual Life Insurance Company in Japan • Incorporated on 25 September 2007 • Got the license for undertaking life insurance business on 26 December 2008 • Shareholding: BOI (48%); Union Bank of India (26%); and Dai-ichi Life (26%) • Foreign and Indian equity capital is Rs. 65 crore and Rs.185 crore, respectively
24	Tata AIA Life Insurance Company Ltd. (Tata AIA Life Insurance Company, About-Tata-Aia available at: http://www.tataaia.com)	• Joint venture between Tata Sons Ltd., one of the leading business groups in India having a long connection with Indian insurance sector, and AIA (American International Assurance) Group Ltd., a leading international insurance and financial services organisation in the USA • Combines the Tata Group's pre-eminent leadership position and AIA's global presence • Permitted to operate in India on 12 February 2001 • Started its operations on 1 April 2001 • Shareholding: Tata Group (74%); AIA (26%) • Foreign and Indian partners hold more than Rs. 500 crores and Rs.1400 crores of capital in the company • Provides insurance solutions to individual and corporate

are compulsory. The Government is therefore supposed to protect the consumers who save their hard earned money through different life insurance products. The Government performs this role with the help of a few Government officials in close connection with a body of expert entrusted with the responsibility of proposing a regulation for reducing malpractices in the market. The Government can fulfil their responsibility efficiently only when the market is well regulated (Trivedi, 2008). Constant supervision of life insurance sector on the basis of the legislation created by the body experts is essential for the social and economical development of the country. Life insurance business operating in India in collaboration with another foreign company does not guarantee fair practice. Hence, they must be strictly regulated to protect the legitimate interest of the insured public. Professional regulations are required for both public and private life insurers particularly in the areas of customer service, claim settlement, resolution of dispute, prevention of restrictive trade practice and investment of life insurance funds. These regulations are set of principles that must be followed to ensure a fair practice. The objectives of the regulator vary from country to country and depend on political philosophy of a country and history of the industry for which regulations are made (Palande et al., 2003). There is no standard model for regulation and every country makes its own depending upon its experience, administrative ability, socio-economic and political attitude. In India, regulations governing life insurance market are made to facilitate development of a healthy life insurance market; protect interest of the policyholders; regulate operations of the life insurers; connect Indian life insurance market with other foreign markets; alert life insurers of mismanagement and insolvency; and instil competition in Indian life insurance market (Pathak, 2006). Prior to 1912, British colonised India had no particular act to regulate life insurance companies. They were mainly governed by the Indian Companies Act, 1882. However, it was not sufficient to control and regulate the life insurance business in India. In the absence of a regulation, life insurance companies went into speculative businesses and some of them failed miserably. Swadeshi Movement in 1905 created indigenous life insurance companies in India. In 1909, the British Parliament passed the British Act, 1909. In India, the British Government also passed two sets of acts based on the British Act, 1909, to provide a better control of life insurance companies in India—(a) the Life Insurance Companies Act, 1912, and the Provident Fund Act, 1912 (Sharma, 2010). Development of select acts relating to insurance sector is discussed in Table 2.3.

Table 2.3 Regulations in the pre-independence era

Sl. No.	Year	Act	Salient points
1	1870	Insurance Act (Kumar, 1991)	• First act on insurance sector • Enacted by the British Government and passed in the British Parliament after failure of number of life insurance companies • Under this law insurers insured the European lives at normal rate but Indian lives with an extra premium of 15–20% • Demand for state control on life insurance companies turned down by the Government on the following grounds: (a) no statistics on Indian lives; (b) difficulty in ascertaining correct age of a person; and (c) difficulty of operation of life insurance business outside the presidency town
2	1883	Indian Companies Act	• No proper act to control life insurance business till the end of nineteenth century • Covered both banking and insurance companies • Regulatory supervision was insufficient • Not focussed on interest of the policyholders or economic development of India

Sl. No.	Year	Act	Salient points
3	1912	Indian Life Insurance Company Act	• First act on Indian life insurance sector and governed life insurance business for 26 years • Not applied for general insurers • Based on the British Act, 1909 • Premium was determined based on rate table and periodical valuation certified by an actuary • Discriminatory (Indian insurers were required to keep a deposit with the Government, but this provision was not applicable in the foreign life insurance companies) • The law restricted the activity of Indian life insurers but not foreign life insurers
4	1928	Indian Insurance Companies Act	• Only significant act in life insurance business before the Insurance Act, 1938 • The act allowed Indian Government to collect statistical information from the Indian life insurers operating in India and other foreign countries, foreign life insurers operating in India and provident insurance societies operating in India • It was observed that foreign life insurers were doing well as compared to the Indian life insurers

(continued)

Table 2.3 (continued)

Sl. No.	Year	Act	Salient points
5	1938	Insurance Act (Cummins & Venard, 2007)	• Modification of the earlier act to regulate the life insurance business for safety and security of the investors • First legislation to ensure strict state control of life insurance business • Entire life insurance sector was brought under the act • Discrimination between Indian and foreign companies was eliminated • Select provisions: (a) avoid speculative condition; (b) compulsory registration of insurance companies; (c) filling return on investment and financial condition with regulatory authorities; (d) constitution of a department of insurance; (e) rebate, licensing of agent, restriction of commission, etc.; (f) periodical valuation of Indian and foreign insurance companies operating in India; (g) standardisation of insurance policy norms; (h) representative of policyholders in Board of Directors (BOD) of the company • Scope of life insurance business to spread in urban and rural areas; malpractices and frequent liquidation of the companies; financial interdependence among the large industrial houses controlling life insurance businesses called for nationalisation of life insurance businesses in 1956. Till then, the act was amended 12 times

2.4.2   Regulatory Framework in the Post-independence Era

In the post-independence era, shortcomings of the previous acts with respect to licensing of agent, maintenance of account, expenses by way of commission and investment of funds were identified, and at different points of times, various amendments were made to the existing Insurance Act, 1938, to rectify those shortcomings (Kumar, 1991). However, malpractices and frequent liquidation of the companies could not be eliminated completely. As a result, policyholders started losing confidence in the sector. Actually, private management controlling the insurance companies then indulged into those illegal activities. Hence, the erstwhile Government of India decided to nationalise the insurance industry.

2.4.2.1   Select Regulations During Nationalisation
Nationalisation of life insurance industry led to the development of the industry and economy as whole. It came into effect by way of a few regulations discussed in Table 2.4.

2.4.3   Regulatory Framework During the Reforms Phase

Industrial policy of 1990 created a pressure on the regulators to reforms life insurance sector facilitate private participation, technology upgradation, customer-oriented product, streamlining investment towards social and rural sector, and infrastructure development. Out of this pressure, the Government formed the Malhotra Committee in 1993 under the chairmanship of Mr. R. N. Malhotra, former Governor, Reserve Bank of India (RBI), in order propose a few recommendations for liberalisation of the sector. The committee submitted its reports in 1994. One of the important recommendations of the committee was diluting the role Controller of Insurance and forming Insurance Regulatory Authority (IRA) for the insurance market, in line with the Securities and Exchange Board of India (SEBI) for the securities market. The IRA Bill, 1996, was introduced in the parliament on 20 December 1996 to regulate and promote systematic growth of the insurance industry. However, the bill was not passed. The bill was again introduced on 5 December 1998. Once again, it was rejected and it was withdrawn by the Government. In the same year, a fresh bill namely Insurance Regulatory and Development Authority (IRDA) bill was introduced incorporating therein certain amendments suggested by the parliamentary standing committee. Now,

Table 2.4 Select regulations during nationalisation

Sl. No.	Year	Act	Salient points
1	1950	The Insurance (Amendment) Act	• In 1945, policyholders started demanding protection of their interest
			• A committee was formed under chairmanship of Shri Cowasji Jehangir to unearth the misconduct in the sector
			• On the basis of the report of the committee, a bill was enacted in the parliament on 18 April 1950
			• According to the bill, the Central Government would control the insurance sector by the Controller of Insurance
			• Non-compliance with the provisions of the bill would bring disciplinary actions

Sl. No.	Year	Act	Salient points
2	1956	Life Insurance Corporation Act (Sharma, 2010)	• The 19 January 1956 was a historic day for nationalisation of life insurance sector • On that day, the management of life insurance business of Indian and foreign life insurance companies and provident societies operating in India was taken over by the Indian Government through the Life Insurance (Emergency Provision) Ordinance • LICI was formed on 1 September 1956 by merging all privately held insurance companies • The act granted the LICI exclusive right to conduct life insurance business in India • LICI was formed as a body corporate • It enjoyed monopoly in Indian life insurance sector till 2000 • The objectives of the act were to provide security to the policyholder; prevent malpractice; spread life insurance business in rural area; and use life fund for national development • The act did not provide any concrete provisions with respect to investment portfolio of life fund

this new bill was passed on 2 December 1999. The President of India signed it in January 2000. The act changed certain provisions of the Insurance Act, 1938, and the LICI Act, 1956. It was brought into effect from 19 April 2000 in order to open the life insurance sector for private participation (Palande et al., 2003). However, in pursuant to the IRDA Act, 1999, IRDAI was set up in India in April 2000. Its key objectives were to promote the healthy competition among the life insurers to ensure lower premium and enhance customer satisfactions. The IRDAI has power to monitor the insurance companies for protection of policyholders' interest. Since 2000, the IRDAI also framed a regulation for registration of insurance companies. In August 2000, when the IRDAI officially started its journey as insurance sector regulator, it allowed the foreign insurance companies to enter into joint ventures with their Indian partners with 26% ownership. However, it was later increased to 49%, the Insurance Laws (Amendment) bill, 2015. Specific functions, developmental roles of the IRDAI and regulations issued during the reforms phase are discussed below.

2.4.3.1   Functions of the IRDAI

The functions of the IRDAI have been specified under section (u/s) 14 of the IRDA Act, 1999. The IRDAI has the duty to regulate the life insurance industry for its systematic growth and ensure financial security of the policyholders. Important functions performed by the IRDAI in this regard are: (a) issuing certificate of registration to a new life insurer; (b) regulating investment portfolio of life funds; (c) protecting policyholders' interests by verifying qualification for intermediaries and actuaries of life insurance companies in accordance with the code of conduct; (d) regulating the surveyors and loss assessors; (e) charging fees applicable in the Insurance Act 1938; (f) investigating into the books of accounts of life insurance companies for possible frauds; (g) regulating premium and expenses on different policies; (h) maintaining margin of solvency for life insurance companies; (i) settling disputes among life insurer, policyholders and intermediaries; (j) specifying the percentage of life insurance business in rural and social sector; (k) specifying the percentage of the premium earned for promoting; and (l) regulating professional organisation (Palande et al., 2003).

2.4.3.2 Developmental Role of IRDAI

The basic aim of the IRDAI is to develop healthy business, protect interest of the policyholders and ensure improvement in service quality. The following developmental roles are played by the IRDAI to ensure the following: (a) fair competition in a monopolistic market; (b) consumer awareness; (c) market study to develop innovative products; (d) sophisticated technology with a database on life insurance business; (e) low managerial expenses; (f) vibrant customer service; (g) development of Actuarial Society of India (ASI), the Insurance Institute of India (III) and the Institute of Surveyor and Loss Assessor (ISLA); (h) introduction of professionals in the business; (i) certain percentage of service in rural and social sector; (j) better incentive for the agent and intermediary; (k) elimination of fraud and misappropriation (Palande et al., 2003).

2.4.3.3 Regulations Issued by the IRDAI During Reforms Phase

Different regulations are made at different times to modify the existing system of life insurance business. These are pointed out in Table 2.5.

2.4.4 Regulatory Framework in the Post-reforms Era

In the aftermath of reforms, the IRDAI and the Central Government have issued certain regulations from time to time that controlled different operations of life insurance companies.

2.4.4.1 Regulations

A chronological list of the regulations with a brief discussion is made in the Table 2.6.

2.4.5 Supporting Regulatory Framework

In addition to the specific regulations discussed above, a few regulatory constituents have been developed over time that helped to reshape the structure of Indian life insurance sector. These are discussed here.

2.4.5.1 Life Insurance Council

Life insurance council has been formed to connect among the various stakeholders of the sector. It mainly coordinates among the insurance companies, Government and other regulatory bodies. It works through several sub-committees that include members from all life insurers. The

Table 2.5 Regulations issued during reforms phase

Sl. No.	Act	Salient points
1	IRDA (Obligation of Insurer to Rural or Social Sector) Regulations, 2000 (Obligation of Insurer to Rural or Social Sector, available at: https://www.irdai.gov.in)	• Life insurance was extended only in urban areas and restricted only to the higher class of the society before independence of India • After independence, acts were made to spread the life business in the rural areas among all sections of the society • As per this regulation, every insurer in life insurance business after the commencement of the IRDA, 1999, has to issue life insurance policies to the rural sector (identified based on population census) and social sector • Percentage of underwritten policies in the rural sector out of total policies of the insurer in the first five years of operation should be 7%, 9%, 12%, 14% and 16%, respectively • Social sector on the other hand includes unorganised and informal sector with economically vulnerable or backward classes and other categories of persons, in both rural and urban areas • In the first five years of their operations, a life insurer has an obligation to cover 5000 lives (first year), 7000 lives (second year), 10,000 lives (third year), 15,000 lives (fourth year), and 20,000 lives (fifth year), respectively • If period of operation is less than 12 months, then in the first year of operation, proportionate percentage (rural sector) or proportionate number of lives (social sector), as the case may be, shall be undertaken • The IRDAI may normally revise the obligation once in every five years

2 EVOLUTION AND REGULATORY FRAMEWORK OF LIFE INSURANCE … 49

Sl. No.	Act	Salient points
2	IRDA (Preparation of Financial Statements and Auditors Reports of Insurance Companies) Regulations, 2000	• The insurers are required to maintain their books of accounts as per the provisions of relevant company law and the Insurance Act, 1938 • These regulations explain the methods and principles for preparation of the financial statements • Balance Sheet, Revenue Account, Receipts and Payments Account and Profit and Loss (P/L) Account of the insurer should be made as per the relevant Accounting Standards (ASs) issued by the Institute of Chartered Accountants of India (ICAI) • The IRDAI may issue guidelines for appointment, continuation or removal of the auditor of the insurer
3	IRDA (Insurance Advertisement and Disclosure) Regulations, 2000	• The regulation is related to advertisement of the insurance product • Every advertisement issued by an insurer is subject to inspection and review by the IRDAI for the content, context, prominence, required disclosures and omission of required information • The insurer should have a compliance officer to deal with this issue • Any change in the advertisement is treated as a new advertisement • If the advertisement is not in accordance with the regulations, the IRDAI is bound to take action • Every insurer is required to follow the provisions with respect to rebate and commission payable to any person u/s 41 of the Insurance Act, 1938

(continued)

Table 2.5 (continued)

Sl. No.	Act	Salient points
4	IRDA (Assets Liabilities and Solvency Margins of Insurance) Regulations, 2000	• Every insurer should prepare a statement on valuation of their assets, their liabilities and their solvency margin in accordance with Schedule-I, Schedule-IIA and Schedule-IIIA, respectively, of this regulations • India has adopted fixed ration model for calculating solvency margin • Financial risk of human life is assessed and managed through this system • The IRDAI also provides the guidelines in this regard

Table 2.6 Regulations issued in the post-reforms era

Sl. No.	Act	Salient Points
1	IRDA (Protection of Policyholder's Interest) Regulations, 2002	• Insurer, agent or any other intermediaries should follow the code of conduct of the IRDAI for the sale of life insurance policy, and they should provide material information regarding the benefits of the policy, relevant terms and conditions of insurance coverage and claim settlement • The IRDAI also provides certain guidelines for protecting interests of the policyholders
2	The Insurance Law (Amendment) Bill, 2008	• As per the IRDAI decision, foreign companies were not allowed to hold more than 26% of the total share of an Indian insurer • The bill was proposed against this decision to increase the limit of foreign holdings to 49% for the insurers with permanent registration • It was introduced in the Rajya Sabha and subsequently referred to the Standing Committee on Finance in 2009 • Finally, it was passed as Insurance Laws (Amendment) Bill, 2015
3	The Life Insurance Corporation (Amendment) Bill, 2009 (Passed in Both Houses) (LICI Bill, 2009 available at: http://164.100.47.4/billstexts)	• The amendment of the existing bill was required to allow the LICI to compete with the private players • It was adopted to raise the level of equity capital of the LICI from Rs. 5 crores to Rs. 100 crores, at par with other private players • It was passed in the parliament in 2011

(continued)

Table 2.6 (continued)

Sl. No.	Act	Salient Points
4	IRDA (Issuance of Capital by Life insurance Companies) Regulations, 2011	• As per the provisions of this regulation, life insurers having an experience of 10 years in the industry may approach the SEBI to raise finance through Initial Public Offer (IPO) subject to prior approval of the IRDA • The approval is valid for one year, within which the company may go for the IPO
5	IRDA (Standard Proposal Form for Life Insurance) Regulations, 2013	• The IRDAI has asked all life insurers to adopt a standard proposal form to seek insurance cover for the policyholders to maintain uniformity and transparency • Format of the proposal form is attached with this regulation It has four parts: (a) details of the prospect; (b) specialised/additional information; (c) suitability analysis; and (d) recommendation • This format is applicable to all individual policies irrespective of the segment and type of product
6	IRDA (Life Insurance-Reinsurance) Regulations, 2013	• The IRDAI has mandated reinsurance of life insurance companies with domestic insurers • Percentage for reinsurance is notified by the IRDAI and this will not exceed 30% of the sum assured • The main objectives of reinsurance programme are to: (a) maximise retention within India; (b) develop adequate capacity; (c) secure the best possible protection; and (d) simplify the business administration

Sl. No.	Act	Salient Points
7	IRDA (Licensing of Banks as Insurance Brokers) Regulations, 2013	• The IRDAI has permitted the banks to act as insurance-brokers and without any fresh capital investment • They can sell life insurance product of more than one insurer in order to increase the insurance sector penetration in the country • The license will remain valid for three years from the date of issue unless it is suspended • Under this system, no remuneration is to be paid to the insurance broker • Every insurance broker has to follow the code of conduct of the IRDAI and maintain separate books of accounts annually for insurance broking business
8	IRDA (Investment) (Fifth Amendment) Regulations, 2013	• The amendment in the regulation facilitates channelisation of long-term savings in Government and debt instrument • The investment assets other than funds relating to pension funds and ULIP funds in the Government, and other approved securities are not less than 50%; investment assets in pension, annuity and group business are not less than 40% and investment assets in unit linked business are not less than 30%
9	Insurance Laws (Amendment) Bill, 2015 (Insurance-Laws-Amendment, Bill, 2015 available at: https://www.indianbarassociation.org)	• The parliament passed the bill to allow the foreign holdings from 26 to 49% maintaining the safeguard of Indian ownership and control • This ceiling is applicable on the paid-up equity capital of the insurance company • This changing landscape is very important for the strategic and financial investment in the insurance industry • As per this amendment, foreign investment up to 26% is under automatic route • Beyond 26% up to 49%, it requires approval from the Foreign Investment Promotion Board of India

council has an executive committee, which consists of 21 members of which two are from the IRDAI and the rest are from the approved life insurers. The objective of the council is to play a significant and complementary role in transforming India's life insurance industry into a vibrant, trustworthy and profitable service and helping people in their journey to prosperity.

2.4.5.2   *Ombudsmen*

As per the Redressal of Public Grievances Rules, 1998, Insurance Ombudsmen are appointed to settle claim from the insurers in a cost-effective manner. The person having grievance against an insurer can complain to the Ombudsmen within the specified jurisdiction. Ombudsmen are empowered to accept and consider the dispute among the parties. It acts as councillor and mediator for settlement of such dispute.

2.4.5.3   *Other Laws Relating to Life Insurance Industry*

Life insurance businesses are influenced by different types of laws and acts such as specified law applicable for the life insurance industry, self-regulations imposed by the industry, professional code of conduct of various professional bodies related to the life insurance business and other general laws applied in India. Apart from the Insurance Act, 1938, the LIC Act, 1956, and the IRDA Act, 1999, a few provisions of some other general laws are also applicable to the life insurance sector. They directly or indirectly regulate the life insurance companies in India (Trivedi, 2008). A few of those laws are: (a) the Carriers Act, 1865; (b) the Indian Contract Act, 1872; (c) Married Women's Property Act, 1874; (d) Indian Post Office Act, 1898; (e) Indian Stamp Act, 1899; (f) Workmen's Compensation Act, 1923; (g) the Indian Succession Act, 1925; (h) Employee's State Insurance Act, 1948; (i) the Hindu Succession Act, 1956; (j) Income Tax Act, 1961; (k) Consumer Protection Act, 1986; (l) Indian Railways Act, 1989; (m) Public Liability Insurance Act, 1991; (n) Securities Exchange Board of India (SEBI) Act, 1992; (o) Foreign Exchange Management Act, 2000; and (p) the Indian Companies Act, 2013.

2.5 INVESTMENT PORTFOLIO OF LIFE INSURANCE INDUSTRY

Investment portfolio of life insurance companies is a framework of investment by the life insurance companies as prescribed by the statutory authorities to provide maximum security to the investment of policyholders as well as maximum return on their investment. Investible funds of life insurance industry are categorised into three parts: (a) life fund, (b) pension, general and group fund and (c) unit linked fund.

The fund mobilised by the life insurance companies and its investment in the productive sector is significant for economic growth. However, initially, the Government of India has not taken any specific policy in this regard. Naturally, large shareholders controlling the management of the insurance companies invested this fund to serve their own purpose. The practice was harmful for the interests of the policyholder and growth of the life insurance sector. In fact, all the acts and regulations made at that time facilitated this misuse of funds (Kumar, 1991). In this section, the development of the regulatory policies with regard to the investment portfolio of life insurance companies is discussed by segmenting it into four eras: (a) pre-independence era; (b) post-independence nationalisation era; (c) post-nationalisation pre-reforms era; and (d) post-reforms era.

2.5.1 Investment Portfolio During Pre-independence Era

Investment portfolio of life funds was fixed by the Government under the Insurance Act, 1938. This was the first wide-ranging act to control 245 insurance companies before the independence. According to the act, insurance companies were required to invest in Indian financial market (u/s 27 and 27A).

Life funds were interlocked between bank and insurance companies to serve their own interest. In 1938, the Government of India introduced a bill in the legislative council to control the malpractice in the life insurance business. The Insurance Act, 1938, was passed after some changes in the original bill. It was the first comprehensive act to strictly control manipulation of funds, operational expenditure of life insurance business. An investment portfolio was prescribed within the framework of this act. However, it was partly changed on the basis of national priority and the emerging market condition. Previously, there was no act to monitor

Table 2.7   Investment portfolio in the pre-independence era

No.	Investment in	Percentage
1	Government securities	Not less than 25%
2	Government or other approved securities	Not less than 25%
3	Other investments, which include loans to State Governments for housing and water supply schemes, Municipal Securities not included in category one, Government-guaranteed loans to Municipal Committee and cooperative sugar factories	Not more than 15%
4	Approved investment, which includes shares and debentures of public and private limited companies of cooperative societies, immovable property, loans to its policyholders and fixed deposits with scheduled banks and cooperative societies	Up to 35%

Source Bhole (2004)

investment of life fund. Indian Government also did not pass any regulation in this regard. As per the provisions of the Insurance Act 1938, the investment portfolio mandated by the Government of India is shown in Table 2.7.

It is observed that around 50% of the total fund is invested in Government and other approved securities to ensure maximum safety of the policyholders' money. Out of the remaining funds, 15% is kept aside for those areas that fulfil primary needs of citizen. Finally, 35% is invested in comparatively risky asset classes to ensure growth in return. Such a portfolio is a good trade-off between risk and return of the policyholders.

2.5.2   Investment Portfolio Post-independence During Nationalisation of Life Insurance Business

After independence but before the nationalisation of life insurance companies, a limited development was made to the already existing investment portfolio. This period was characterised by malpractices, deficiencies and frequent liquidation of insurance companies. It led to lack of public confidence in security funds mobilised from the policyholders. For this reason, Sir Cowasji Jehangir Committee was formed in April 1945 to enquire into the undesirable developments in the management of insurance companies in India and to check the manipulation of funds. The committee recommended some amendments in the provisions of the Insurance Act, 1938. The bill was introduced in April 1950 and passed as the Insurance

Act, 1950, in the Indian Parliament. The investment portfolio as per the Insurance Act, 1950, was as shown in Table 2.8.

It shows that 50% of assets are invested in the Government and other approved securities to ensure security of the policyholders fund. At the same time, 35% of the fund is invested in stocks and bonds of the blue chip companies to ensure stable rate of return on the investment. Investment in other areas decided by the BOD of the respective companies is restricted to 15% of the fund. It denotes that some power of the investment had been handed over to the management of the life insurance company.

The portfolio also ensures a good trade-off between risk and return. However, unscrupulous personnel misused the portion allotted to them to serve their own purposes, which was unhealthy for the growth of the sector. Hence, based on public demand, the erstwhile Government considered the proposal for nationalisation of life insurance companies. Actually, the Indian Government wanted to increase market penetration by the life insurance companies and use its resources for economic development. Inefficient management of the life insurers was coming in the way of Government's plan. Moreover, during pre-independence era, insurance industry in India had monopolistic exploitation, poor customer service, high premium rate, low productivity, lesser application of technology and limited available of products (Bhasin, 2007). All these aspects together made the Government to go for nationalisation of the LICI.

Table 2.8 Investment portfolio during nationalisation

No.	Investment in	Percentage of total fund
1	Government securities	25%
2	Government and other approved securities	25%
3	Approved investment that includes stocks and bonds of publicly traded companies (but they should be blue chip companies)	35%
4	Investment in other areas if the board of directors of the insurance company approved them	15%

Source: Palande et al. (2003)

2.5.3   Investment Portfolio Post-nationalisation and Pre-reforms Era

Life insurance business was nationalised on 1 September 1956 with the signature of the President of India, and all the life insurance companies were brought under the LICI. Following liberalisation, before reforms, investment policy of the LICI has been changed several times (Table 2.9).

After nationalisation in 1956, the Insurance Act, 1938, was applicable with some modifications. When financial reforms started in 1993, reorganisation of the investment portfolio of the LICI was one of the important agendas. The Government of India appointed the Malhotra Committee in April 1993 and the committee submitted its recommendation in January 1999. One of the recommendations was the investment portfolio of life insurance companies. It was implemented with effect from 2001.

2.5.4   Investment Portfolio of Life Insurance Industry After Reforms

Financial sector reforms took place in 1993 and reforms in life insurance sector became a priority in it to provide better services to the policyholders. Competition in the sector was introduced by opening the sector to the private and foreign players. In 2000, the IRDAI was formed as per Malhotra Committee recommendation. It allowed reduction in mandated investment and greater portfolio diversification for better return on investment (Saha, 2021). Accordingly, total fund of the life insurance companies has been categorised into three heads: (a) life fund; (b) pension and annuity fund; and (c) unit linked fund. Investment portfolio of these three types of funds is governed as per Insurance Regulations and Development (Investment) Regulations, 2000. It was amended twice in 2001 and 2013. Investment portfolio of life fund as per IRDA regulations and its subsequent amendments are discussed in Table 2.10.

While in Government securities were restricted to 25% of life funds, from 2013, the restriction was withdrawn. Approved investment has been introduced as a separate category from 2013. In 2000 regulation, maximum limit for other investment was 20%, which was increased to 35% in 2001. However, from 2013, the limit was once again reduced to 15%. Now, the investment portfolio of pension and general annuity fund

Table 2.9 Investment policy of the LICI in the post-nationalisation era

Sl. No.	Recommended by	Important dates	No.	Investment in	Percentage of total funds	Focus area
1	Investment Committee, LICI in their board meetings (Kumar, 1991)	11 July 1958 (final decision taken); 25 August 1958 (date of modification of Insurance Act 1938)	1	Government and approved securities, which are generally gilt-edged securities	≥ 50%	• Investment in stock or bond issued by a company having strong record of consistent earnings and dividend with low risk
			2	Investments approved under this section	35%	• Stable rate of return
			3	Other investments	≤ 15%	• Importance to the social sector
2	Investment Committee, LICI (by modification of Sec. 27A, Insurance Act 1938) (Cummines and Venard, 2007)	1958	1	Central Government market securities	≥ 20%	• Consistency of return
			2	Loans to National Housing Bank including (1) above	≥ 25%	• Security of life insurance fund

(continued)

Table 2.9 (continued)

Sl. No.	Recommended by	Important dates	No.	Investment in	Percentage of total funds	Focus area
			3	State Government securities, including (2) above	≥ 50%	
			4	Socially oriented sectors including the public sector, the cooperative sector, house building by policyholders and own-home schemes including (3) above	≥ 75%	
3	Informal Group constituted by the Central Government under the chairmanship of former RBI Governor Mr. S. Jagannathan (Kumar, 1991)	1970 (committee was formed); 1971 (committee proposed its recommendation); 7 November 1974 (date of implementation)	1	Government of India marketable securities	≥ 25%	• Investment in social sector and other sector • More than 50% fund in Government and approved sector; • Priority to social schemes (e.g. OYH) • Inconsistent with the objective of consistent return for policyholders

Sl. No.	Recommended by	Important dates	No.	Investment in	Percentage of total funds	Focus area
			2	Central and State Government securities including Government-guaranteed marketable securities, and including (1) above	≥ 50%	
			3	In socially oriented sector, including public sector, cooperative sector, house building by policyholders, Own Your Home (OYH) schemes including (2) above	≥ 75%	
			4	Loan on policies; investment to private sector; construction and acquisition of properties; funds in pipeline not available for investment	25%	
4	Jagannathan Committee (Bhattacharyya, 2004)	1975 (date of recommendation by the committee)	1	In Central Government marketable securities	≥ 25%	• Maximum security and moderate return • More than 50% in Government securities • 25% in other sectors • Priority to social sectors

(continued)

Table 2.9 (continued)

Sl. No.	Recommended by	Important dates	No.	Investment in	Percentage of total funds	Focus area
			2	In Central Government, State Government securities, including the Government-guaranteed Marketable Securities including (1) above	≥ 50%	
			3	In social-oriented sector including public sector cooperative sector, Own Your Home (OYH) scheme including (2) above	≥ 75%	
			4	Loan against surrender value of the policies	8%	
			5	Immovable properties	2%	
			6	Private sector investment	10%	
			7	Funds in the pipeline not available for investment	5%	
5	Era Sezhiyan Committee under the chairmanship of Mr. Mr. Era Sezhiyan (Kumar, 1991)	18 May 1979 (committee was constituted); October 1980 (issued for implementation)	1	Central and State Government securities	20%	• Reduction in the investment towards Government securities • Investment in social sector at market rate • Less manipulation with respect to interest

Sl. No.	Recommended by	Important dates	No.	Investment in	Percentage of total funds	Focus area
			2	Approved marketable securities	20%	
			3	Socially oriented sector at market rate of interest (0.5% to be kept by the Government as guarantee)	25%	
6	Investment Committee, LICI (modified the recommendations by Era Sezhiyan Committee) (Kumar, 1991)	1995	1	Central Government Marketable Securities	≥ 20%	• More than 50% in Government securities to ensure security of fund • Investment in social sector to improve standard of living
			2	Loans to housing bank including (1) above	≥ 25%	
			3	State Government securities including Government Marketable Securities, inclusive of (2) above	≥ 50%	
			4	Socially oriented sectors including public sector, cooperative sector house building by policyholders, own your house scheme, inclusive of (3) above	≥ 75%	
			5	Private corporate sector, loans to policyholders for construction and acquisition of immovable property	25%	

Table 2.10 Investment portfolio of life fund

No.	Investment in	Percentage of life fund		
		Regulations 2000	Amendment 2001	Amendment 2013
1	Government securities	25%	25%	≥ 25%
2	Government securities or other approved securities including (1) above	≥ 50%	≥ 50%	≥ 50%
3	Approved investment	–	–	≤ 50%
4	Infrastructure investment (in housing and social sector)	≥ 15%	≥ 15%	≥ 15%
5	Other investments (governed by exposure/prudential norms)	≤ 20%	≤ 35%	≤ 15%
6	Other than approved investment governed by exposure/prudential norms	≤ 15%	–	–

Source IRDA, (Investment), Regulations 2000 (up to Amendment in 2013) available at: https://www.irdai.gov.in

in accordance with 2000 regulations and its subsequent amendment are discussed (Table 2.11).

Investment in Government securities was restricted up to 20% in 2000 regulation. However, it was relaxed from 2001 amendment. The portfolio is more focussed towards ensuring safety and security of returns. ULIP was introduced in the life insurance business from 2001. Hence, investment portfolio of the ULIP fund as per 2001 and 2013 amendment of IRD (Investment) Regulations is discussed (Table 2.12).

Insurers have a relaxation with respect to investment of ULIP fund in approved and other than approved investments.

2.6   Conclusion

Life insurance companies, its governing regulations and its investment portfolio of controlled funds have been gradually evolving since pre-independence era. Before independence, Indian life insurance industry

Table 2.11   Investment portfolio of pension and annuity fund

No.	Investment in	Percentage of life fund		
		Regulations 2000	Amendment 2001	Amendment 2013
1	Government securities	20%	≥ 20%	≥ 20%
2	Government securities or other approved securities inclusive of (1) above	≥ 40%	≥ 40%	≥ 40%
3	Balance to be invested in approved investments	≤ 60%	≤ 60%	≤ 60%

Source IRDA, (Investment), Regulations 2000 (up to Amendment in 2013) available at: https://www.irdai.gov.in

Table 2.12   Investment portfolio of ULIP fund

No.	Investment in	Percentage of life fund	
		Amendment 2001	Amendment 2013
1	Approved investments	≥ 75%	≥ 75%
2	Other than approved investments	≤ 25%	≤ 25%

Source IRDA, (Investment), Regulations 2000 (up to Amendment in 2013) available at: https://www.irdai.gov.in

was dominated by mainly British life insurance companies and the applicable regulations were made keeping in view their interest. Back then, it was an urban phenomenon. After India's independence, nationalisation of the LICI by bringing together numerous small insurance companies was a significant event in India's life insurance history. It led to a surge in premium mobilisation and investible fund. However, in pre-reforms era, the LICI enjoyed complete monopoly in the sector. After financial sector reforms, private participation, technology up-gradation, numerous products and after sale service have enhanced the efficiency of the life insurance sector. New market-oriented products, such as ULIP, were introduced to tap a potential market looking for increased return on investment. Private players were allowed to partner with foreign companies. The entire life insurance sector was brought under the ambit of the IRDAI. The IRDAI has increased penetration of life insurance in rural sector as well. Along with other parameters, the IRDAI has also regulated the total fund of the life insurance companies into three segments, like life fund, pension and annuity fund, and ULIP fund. In the pre-reforms era, investments were made in Government and approved securities, while it has been extended to infrastructure and social sectors in the post-reforms era.

In the following chapter, the performance of the LICI and select other private life insurance companies during post-reforms era has been analysed with regard to premium mobilisation, total investment and sector-wise investment.

REFERENCES

Aegon Religare Life insurance Company. *History of company*. Retrieved from AEGON RELIGARE Website: http://www.aegonreligare.com

Aviva Life Insurance Company. *History of company*. Retrieved from AVIVA INDIA Website: http://www.avivaindia.com

Bajaj Allianz Life Insurance Company. *History of company*. Retrieved from BAJAJ ALLIANZ Website: http://www.bajajallianz.com

Bharti AXA Life Insurance Company. *History of company*. Retrieved from BHIRTI AXALIFE Website: https://www.bharti-axalife.com

Bhasin, N. (2007). *Banking and financial market in India 1947 to 2007*. Century Publication.

Bhattacharyya, R. K. (2004). *Money and financial system*. Kolkata: Bhattacharjee Brothers

Bhole, L. M. (2004). *Financial institutions and market*. New Delhi: Tata McGraw Hill.

Birla Life Insurance Company. *History of company*. Retrieved from Insurance BIRLA SUNLIFE INSURANCE Website: http://insurance.birlasunlife.com

Cummins, D., & Venard, B. (2007). *Handbook of international insurance between global dynamics and local contingencies*. Springer.

DHFL Pramerica Life Insurance Company. *History of company*. Retrieved from DHFL PRAMERICA Website: https://www.dhflpramerica.com

Edelweiss Tokio Life insurance Company. *History of company*. Retrieved from EDELWEISS TOKIO Website: http://www.edelweisstokio.in

Exide Life Insurance Company. *History of company*. Retrieved from EXIDE LIFE Website: http://www.exidelife.in

Future Generali India Life Insurance Company. *History of company*. Retrieved from FUTURE GENERALI Website: http://www.futuregenerali.in

Gopalakrishana, D. (2010). The philosophy of life insurance. *The Journal of Insurance Institute of India, XXXVI*, 75–81.

HDFC Standard Life Insurance Company. *History of company.* Retrieved from HDFC LIFE Website: http://www.hdfclife.com

ICICI Prudential Life Insurance. *History of company.* Retrieved from ICICI PRULIFE Website: http://www.iciciprulife.com

IDBI Federal Life Issuance Company. *History of company.* Retrieved from IDBI FEDERAL Website: http://www.idbifederal.com

India First Life Insurance Company. *History of company.* Retrieved From INDIAFIRST LIFE Website: http://www.indiafirstlife.com

Insurance Law Bill. *Amendment Bill, 2008.* Retrieved from INDIAN BAR ASSOCIATION Website: https://www.indianbarassociation.org

Insurance Laws. *Amendment Bill, 2015.* Retrieved from INDIAN BAR ASSOCIATION Website: https://www.indianbarassociation.org

Insurer Regulations. *About IRDA.* Retrieved from SHODHGANGA Website: http://shodhganga.inflibnet.ac.in

IRDA, (Investment) (Amendment), Regulations, 2013.

IRDA, (Investment) Regulations, 2000.

IRDA, Annual Report, 2013–2014.

Khan, M. Y. (2006). *Indian financial system.* Tata McGraw Hill.

Kotak Mahindra Old Mutual Life Insurance Company. *History of company.* Retrieved from INSURANCE KOTAK Website: http://insurance.kotak.com

Kumar, D. (1991). *Tryst with trust: The LIC story.* Mumbai: LIC of India.

Life Insurance Company. *Overview of life insurance company.* Retrieved from SHODHGANGA Website: http://shodhganga.inflibnet.ac.in

Life Insurance Corporation Bill. *Amendment Bill, 2009.* Retrieved from BILL-TEXTS Website: http://164.100.47.4/billstexts/lsbilltexts/PassedBothHouses/LIC.

Max Life Insurance Company. *History of company.* Retrieved from MAXLIFEINSURANCE Website: http://www.maxlifeinsurance.com

Obligation of Insurer. *IRDA Regulations, 2000.* Retrieved from IRDA Website: https://www.irdai.gov.in

Overview of life Insurance company. *Brief Study.* Retrieved from SHODHGANGA Website: http://shodhganga.inflibnet.ac.in

Palande, P. S., Shah, R. S., & Lunawat, M. L. (2003). *Insurance India changing policies and emerging opportunities.* Response Books.

Pathak, B. V. (2006). *The Indian financial system.* New Delhi: Pearson Education

PNB MetLife India Insurance Company. *History of company.* Retrieved from PNB METLIFE Website: http://www.pnbmetlife.com

Reliance Life Insurance Company. *History of company.* Retrieved from RELIANCE LIFE Website: http://www.reliancelife.com

Saha, S. S. (2021). *Indian financial system: Financial markets, institutions and services* (2nd ed.). Tata McGraw Hill.

Sahara India Life Insurance Company. *History of company.* Retrieved from SHODHGANGA Website: http://shodhganga.inflibnet.ac.in

SBI Life Insurance Company. *History of company.* Retrieved from SBI LIFE Website: http://www.sbilife.co.in

Sharma, R. (2010). *Insurance.* Agra: Lakshmi Narain Agarwal.

Shriram Life Insurance Company. *History of company.* Retrieved from SHRIM LIFE Website: http://www.shriramlife.com

Sinha, A., & Gandhi, S. K. (2014). *Financial performance analysis of life insurers in India.* Scholar's Press.

Star Union Dai-Ichi Life Insurance Company. *History of company.* Retrieved from SUD LIFE Website: https://www.sudlife.in

Tata AIA Life Insurance Company. *History of company.* Retrieved from TATA AIA Website: http://www.tataaia.co

Trivedi, P., R. (2008). *Encyclopaedia of insurance business and management.* Nagaland: Janada, Prakashan.

www.irdai.gov.in

Premium Mobilisation and Investment Portfolio by the LICI and Select Private Life Insurance Companies: An Analytical Study

Abstract An attempt has been made, in this chapter, to critically analyse the growths and trends in premium mobilisation and investment portfolio of the Life Insurance Corporation of India (LICI) and six select private life insurance companies (PLICs) in the post-reforms era. It has been observed that in almost all the parameters, LICI has outperformed its private peers. However, LICI's progress over the years is slow-paced. The compounded annual growth rate (CAGR) of LICI is also the least among the sample selected. Among the PLICs, SBI Life (SBI), Bajaj Allianz (BAJAJ) and HDFC Life (HDFC) were the front runners. While ICICI Prudential Life (ICICI) lagged behind select PLICSs, it is projecting a positive trend in most of the parameters. Among the PLICs, the SBI has secured the top position while Aditya Birla Sun Life (BIRLA) was among the least performers. Correlation between premium collection and total investments based on Pearson's correlation coefficient technique suggests that premium collection and total investments of all companies barring Bajaj Allianz are positively and significantly correlated. Companies also have significant positive correlation among themselves in terms of premium collection, total investments and other sectorial investments.

© The Author(s), under exclusive license to Springer Nature
Singapore Pte Ltd. 2022
S. P. Patra et al., *Investment Pattern of LICI and Select Private LICs
in the Post-reforms Era in India*,
https://doi.org/10.1007/978-981-19-2799-7_3

Keywords Premium Mobilisation · Total Investment · Sectorial Investment · LICI · SBI · BAJAJ · HDFC · Growth · Trend · Pearson's correlation coefficient

3.1   INTRODUCTION

In the previous chapter, Chapter 2, the evolution and regulatory framework of life insurance industry has been discussed. Now, this chapter incorporates an analysis on insurance premium mobilisation and investment portfolio of the Life Insurance Corporation of India (LICI) and six select private life insurance companies. Truly speaking, the insurance companies collect premium from investors by selling different life insurance products and make annual savings of premium collection after settling various expenditures and claims. These annual savings grow into a massive fund for investment. These funds are invested in different investment instruments under different sectors, such as public sector, private sector, joint sector and cooperative sector investment as per Insurance Act. The proportion of the investment, which is known as portfolio investment of the LICI, has been changed over the years considering the return on the investment, safety and security for the interest of the policyholders. Managing investment portfolio is a balance between availability of investment options and alertness to meet prospective large payments. However, in this chapter, an attempt has been made to analyse the growth, trend and correlation of total premium collection, total investment and investment portfolio of the LICI and six select private life insurance companies during the post-reforms era.

3.2   OBJECTIVES

The specific objectives of the chapter are as follows.

3.2.1   Growth Analysis

i. To analyse growth of premium collection by the LICI and six select private life insurance companies during the study period;

ii. To examine growth of total investments by the LICI and six select private life insurance companies during the study period;

iii. To explore growth of investment portfolio of the LICI and six select private life insurance companies during the study period.

3.2.2   Trend Analysis

i. To study trend of premium collection by the LICI and six select private life insurance companies during the study period;

ii. To explore trend of total investments by the LICI and six select private life insurance companies during the study period;

iii. To analyse trend of investment portfolio of the LICI and six select private life insurance companies during the study period;

3.2.3   Correlation Analysis

i. To examine the correlation between growth of premium collection and growth of total investments for each select life insurance companies;

ii. To explore the pair-wise correlation among seven select life insurance companies in terms of growth of premium collection, total investments and investment portfolio during the study period.

3.3   METHODOLOGY

The present study is exploratory in nature. The data for total premium mobilisation, total investment and investment portfolio of the LICI and six select private life insurance companies are collected from the article, text book and annual report of the LICI, IRDAI and RBI (Reserve Bank of India), Handbook of Insurance Statistics and RBI website for 2004–2005 to 2013–2014 (period of study). Data sets are secondary in nature. SPSS 20.0 and MS Excel 2007 are used to analyse those secondary data sets. The statistical tests on different parameters with objectives are mentioned here.

No	Objectives	Statistical Tools
3.2.1	**Growth Analysis**	
	To analyse growth of premium collection by the LICI and six select private life insurance companies during the study period	Year-Wise Growth Analysis
	To analyse growth of total investments by the LICI and six select private life insurance companies during the study period	
	To analyse growth of investment portfolio of the LICI and six select private life insurance companies during the study period	
3.2.2	**Trend Analysis**	
	To analyse trend of premium collection by the LICI and six select private life insurance companies during the study period	Log-linear Model
	To analyse trend of total investments by the LICI and six select private life insurance companies during the study period	
	To analyse trend of investment portfolio of the LICI and six select private life insurance companies during the study period	
3.2.3	**Correlation Analysis**	
	To analyse the correlation between growth of premium collection and growth of total investments for each select life insurance companies	Pearson's Correlation Coefficient and t-test
	To analyse the pair-wise correlation among seven select life insurance companies in terms of growth of premium collection, total investments and investment portfolio during the study period	

3.4   ANALYSIS AND FINDINGS

In this segment, an empirical analysis considering secondary data is made to address the objectives of the study. The analysis and test result are discussed here:

3.4.1   Growth Analysis

Annual growth of a variable is calculated based on the following equation:

$$\Rightarrow Growth(G) = (\text{Ending Value} - \text{Beginning Value}) \div \text{Beginning Value} \times 100$$
$$\Rightarrow G = (Y_t - Y_{t-1}) \div Y_{t-1} \times 100$$

where

- Y_t = Value in year t;
- Y_{t-1} = Value in year Y_{t-1}.

3.4.1.1   Growth of Premium Collection

Premium collection of life insurance companies is very essential to carry on the life insurance business. Principal cash inflow of life insurance business depends on the collection of the premium. It is the life blood to run the life insurance business. Total premium collection comprises first year premium, renewal premium and single year premium. Here, growth of total premium collection of the LICI and select private life insurance companies is analysed during the study period 2004–2005 to 2014–2015. Total premium collection of the LICI and select other private life insurance companies during the period 2004–2005 to 2014–2015 is shown in Table 3.1.

Table 3.1   Total premium collection (As on 31st March) (Rs. in Crores)

Year	LICI	ICICI	BAJAJ	SBI	HDFC	BIRLA	MAX
2004–2005	75,127	2363.82	1001.68	601.18	686.63	915.47	413.43
2005–2006	90,792	4261.05	3133.58	1075.32	1569.91	1259.68	788.13
2006–2007	127,823	7912.99	5345.24	2928.49	2855.87	1776.71	1500.28
2007–2008	149,791	13,561.1	9725.31	5622.14	4858.56	3272.19	2714.6
2008–2009	157,288	15,356.2	10,624.5	7212.1	5564.69	4571.8	3857.26
2009–2010	186,077	16,528.8	11,419.7	10,104	7005.1	5505.66	4860.54
2010–2011	203,473	17,880.6	9609.95	12,945.3	9004.17	5677.07	5812.63
2011–2012	202,889	14,021.6	7488.8	13,133.7	10,202.4	5885.36	6390.53
2012–2013	208,804	13,538.2	6892.7	10,450	11,322.7	5216.3	6638.7
2013–2014	236,942	12,428.7	5843.14	10,728.6	12,062.9	4833.05	7278.54
Total	1,639,006	117,853	71,084.6	74,800.9	65,132.9	38,913.3	40,254.6

Source IRDAI Handbook of Statistics (IRDAI, 2012, 2015)

Now, the growth in premium collection of the LICI and select other private life insurers based on their total premium mobilisation (Table 3.2) is shown below.

Table 3.2 is graphically represented as follows (Chart 3.1).

Findings

Table 3.2 Growth in total premium collection (%)

Year	LICI	ICICI	BAJAJ	SBI	HDFC	BIRLA	MAX
2005–2006	20.85	80.26	212.83	78.87	128.64	37.60	90.63
2006–2007	40.79	85.71	70.58	172.34	81.91	41.04	90.36
2007–2008	17.19	71.38	81.94	91.98	70.13	84.17	80.94
2008–2009	5.00	13.24	9.25	28.28	14.53	39.72	42.09
2009–2010	18.30	7.64	7.48	40.10	25.88	20.43	26.01
2010–2011	9.35	8.18	−15.85	28.12	28.54	3.11	19.59
2011–2012	−0.29	−21.58	−22.12	1.46	13.31	3.67	9.94
2012–2013	2.92	−3.45	−7.90	−20.43	10.98	−11.37	3.88
2013–2014	13.48	−8.20	−15.23	2.76	6.54	−7.35	9.64
Average	15.96	25.91	35.67	47.05	42.27	23.45	41.45

Source Compilation on the basis of Table 3.1 using MS Excel 2007

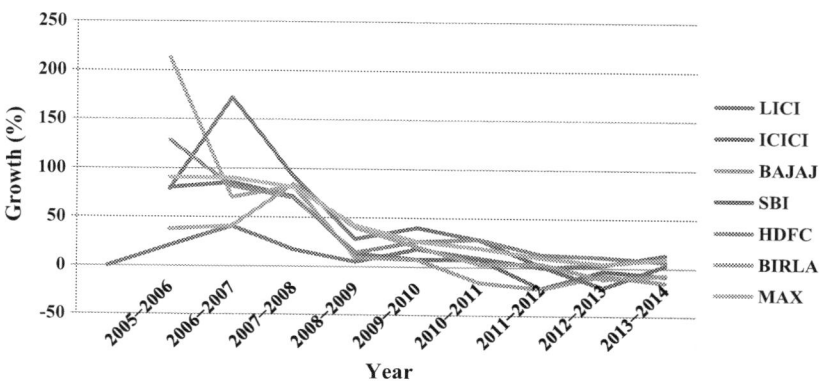

Chart 3.1 Growth of total premium collection (*Source* Compiled based on Table 3.2 using MS Excel)

- During post-reforms period, premium collection of the LICI was very tough due to open up of life insurance sector for private participation. The LICI had to compete with the private life insurance companies in life insurance business.
- Average growth of the premium collection of the LICI during the study period was 15.96%. The growth of premium collection of the LICI was decreased over the years because of participation of private players.
- Average growth of the annual premium collection for the ICICI, BAJAJ, SBI, HDFC, BIRLA and MAX was 25.91%, 35.67%, 47.05%, 42.27%, 23.45% and 41.45%, respectively. This happened because of different premium collections from different life insurance products and different selling strategies of individual private life insurance companies. No negative growth is found in the HDFC and MAX life insurance companies during study period.

3.4.1.2   Growth of Total Investment

In this section, an attempt has been made to examine the annual growth of total investment of the LICI and select other private life insurance companies during post-reforms era using the methodology as adopted previously. Total investments made by the companies during the study period are shown in Table 3.3.

Table 3.3   Total Investment (As on 31st March) (Rs. in Crores)

Year	LICI	ICICI	BAJAJ	SBI	HDFC	BIRLA	MAX
2004–2005	393,185	3474.43	762.07	1054.17	923.35	1295.85	478.09
2005–2006	487,227	7485.50	3324.36	2034.98	2596.29	2350.85	885.85
2006–2007	521,735	14,298.73	6331.18	4515.70	4975.68	3751.57	1839.92
2007–2008	635,748	26,398.33	12,883.55	10,026.72	8929.36	6797.55	3587.01
2008–2009	762,892	32,690.79	17,163.55	14,439.99	10,296.09	8813.04	5564.44
2009–2010	918,247	56,963.07	33,435.26	28,576.58	20,411.47	15,738.31	10,120.96
2010–2011	1,070,276	67,712.89	39,344.69	40,107.23	26,497.80	19,655.76	13,836.42
2011–2012	1,203,818	70,103.21	39,434.38	46,528.15	32,253.67	20,995.49	17,215.06
2012–2013	1,348,996	73,370.51	37,977.98	51,818.86	40,107.83	22,779.33	20,457.88
2013–2014	1,511,133	79,399.45	38,612.83	58,195.20	50,253.39	24,676.59	24,633.00
Total	8,853,257	431,897	229,270	257,298	197,245	126,854	98,618.6

Source IRDAI Handbook of Statistics (IRDAI, 2012, 2015)

Annual growth of total investment of the LICI and other private life insurance companies is shown in Table 3.4 (Chart 3.2).

Findings

- The average growth of the total investment of the LICI during the study period was 16.26%. Average growth of the LICI was decreasing during the period due to life insurance reforms and entry of the private players in life insurance business. Total investment of the LICI was Rs. 467,175 crores during the study period.

Table 3.4   Growth in total investment (%)

Year	LICI	ICICI	BAJAJ	SBI	HDFC	BIRLA	MAX
2005–2006	23.92	115.45	93.04	336.23	181.18	81.41	85.29
2006–2007	07.08	91.02	121.90	90.45	91.65	59.58	107.70
2007–2008	21.85	84.62	122.04	103.49	79.46	81.19	94.95
2008–2009	20.00	23.84	44.02	33.22	15.31	29.65	55.13
2009–2010	20.36	74.25	97.90	94.80	98.24	78.58	81.89
2010–2011	16.56	18.87	40.35	17.67	29.82	24.89	36.71
2011–2012	12.48	3.53	16.01	0.23	21.72	6.82	24.42
2012–2013	12.06	4.66	11.37	−3.69	24.35	8.50	18.84
2013–2014	12.02	8.22	12.31	1.67	25.30	8.33	20.41
Average	16.26	47.16	62.10	74.90	63.00	42.11	58.37

Source Compilation on the basis of Table 3.3 using MS Excel 2007

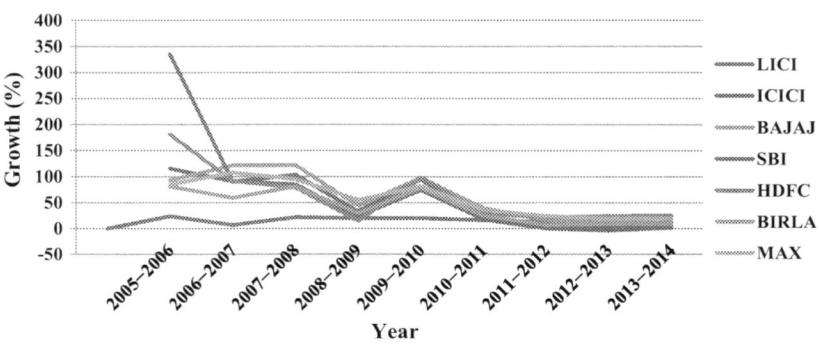

Chart 3.2   Growth in Total Investment (*Source* Compiled based on Table 3.4 using MS Excel)

- Average growth of the total investment for ICICI, BAJAJ, SBI, HDFC, BIRLA and MAX was 47.16%, 62.10%, 74.90%, 63.00%, 42.11% and 58.37%, respectively, because of different premium collection and return on their investment in the financial market. During the study period, total investments of ICICI, BAJAJ, SBI, HDFC, BIRLA and MAX were Rs. 431,897 crore, Rs. 229,270 crore, Rs. 257,298 crore, Rs. 197,245 crore, Rs. 126,854 crore and Rs. 98,619 crore, respectively.

3.4.1.3   *Growth of Sector-Wise Investment*

Investments by life insurance companies can be categorised under four groups: (a) Investment in Government and Other Approved Securities (IGOAS); (b) Infrastructure Investment (II); (c) Approved Investment (AI); and (d) Other than Approved Investment (OAI). Investment in Government and Other Approved Securities (IGOAS) is the sum total of investment in Central Government securities and State Government and other approved securities. These two sectors are combined as Investment in Government and Other Approved Securities (IGOAS) because of non-availability of data separately for two sectors (Central Government securities, and State Government and other approved securities) during the period 2004–2005 to 2006–2007. IGOAS during the study period is shown in Table 3.5

Table 3.5   Investment in government and other approved securities (As on 31st March) (Rs. in Crores)

Year	LICI	ICICI	BAJAJ	SBI	HDFC	BIRLA	MAX
2004–2005	249,287.57	674.69	244.07	647.34	403.66	110.84	335.38
2005–2006	291,216.22	868.17	429.16	851.42	679.21	142.10	524.52
2006–2007	327,392.46	1260.13	657.68	1193.57	932.82	193.49	732.32
2007–2008	369,723.63	1813.51	1395.78	2630.04	1406.95	301.05	1069.98
2008–2009	407,203.20	2248.87	1730.89	3743.10	1586.99	498.95	1610.53
2009–2010	474,589.60	3117.14	2719.98	5420.89	2546.85	806.36	2186.85
2010–2011	563,475.90	4624.02	3349.20	7027.13	3217.53	1190.67	3104.52
2011–2012	640,847.40	5203.58	4858.01	9013.72	4344.38	1582.75	4219.94
2012–2013	719,510.67	7600.43	6941.33	12,467.34	5893.25	1873.27	5956.17
2013–2014	945,743.30	9354.92	9730.21	15,729.07	8027.17	2065.58	8816.00
Total	4,988,989.95	36,765.46	32,056.31	58,723.62	29,038.81	8765.06	28,556.21

Source IRDAI Handbook of Statistics (IRDAI, 2012, 2015)

Table 3.6 Growth of investment in government and other approved securities (%)

Year	LICI	ICICI	BAJAJ	SBI	HDFC	BIRLA	MAX
2005–2006	16.82	28.68	75.83	31.53	68.26	28.20	56.40
2006–2007	12.42	45.15	53.25	40.19	37.34	36.16	39.62
2007–2008	12.93	43.91	112.23	120.35	50.83	55.59	46.11
2008–2009	10.14	24.01	24.01	42.32	12.80	65.74	50.52
2009–2010	16.55	38.61	57.14	44.82	60.48	61.61	35.78
2010–2011	18.73	48.34	23.13	29.63	26.33	47.66	41.96
2011–2012	13.73	12.53	45.05	28.27	35.02	32.93	35.93
2012–2013	12.27	46.06	42.88	38.32	35.65	18.36	41.14
2013–2014	31.44	23.08	40.18	26.16	36.21	10.27	48.01
Average	57.26	34.49	52.63	44.62	40.33	39.61	43.94

Source Compilation on the basis of Table 3.5 using MS Excel 2007

Growth of IGOAS during the study period is shown in Table 3.6. The result of Table 3.6 is shown in Chart 3.3.

Findings

- Growth in the IGOAS for BAJAJ and SBI surged to a significant extent in 2007–2008. Insurance companies turned towards IGOAS

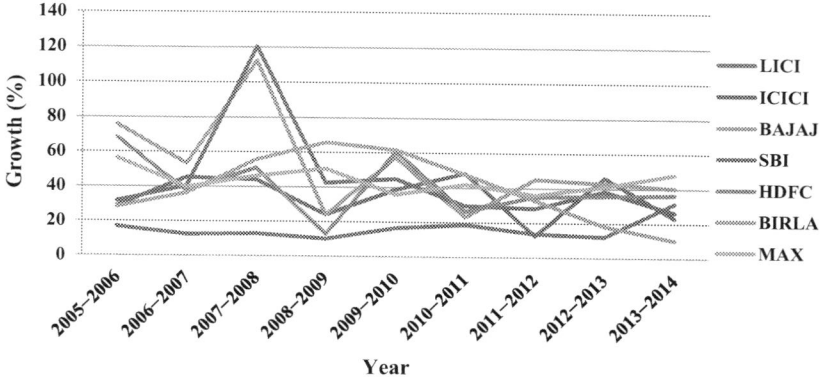

Chart 3.3 Growth of investment in government and other approved securities (*Source* Compiled based on Table 3.6 using MS Excel)

more probably because of uncertainties roaming around private sector at the verge of global economic recession. LICI maintained a steady growth during the period, while that of ICICI and HDFC was very volatile during the period.

- The average growth of LICI was the highest (57.26%) followed by BAJAJ. The average growth of ICICI (34.49%) was least during the study period.

Infrastructure investment by select insurance companies is shown in Table 3.7.

Growth in infrastructure investment during the study period is shown in Table 3.8.

The result of Table 3.8 is shown in Chart 3.4.

Table 3.7   Infrastructure Investment (As on 31st March) (Rs. in Crores)

Year	LICI	ICICI	BAJAJ	SBI	HDFC	BIRLA	MAX
2004–2005	44,660.40	159.04	74.02	155.26	85.80	31.74	89.08
2005–2006	48,182.22	226.11	141.91	264.96	213.28	41.97	130.90
2006–2007	67,616.17	308.39	245.35	400.19	250.86	74.40	238.93
2007–2008	59,715.45	452.08	404.53	652.02	364.77	137.54	429.41
2008–2009	62,065.43	526.27	510.40	663.98	496.61	211.37	504.84
2009–2010	78,991.01	688.31	1045.11	775.20	843.82	414.21	765.19
2010–2011	80,491.49	1080.84	1081.98	746.50	1301.75	535.32	1131.22
2011–2012	84,532.45	1686.00	1614.18	1104.88	1636.71	810.11	1779.46
2012–2013	102,000.90	2418.10	2024.46	1398.19	2038.39	815.73	2152.29
2013–2014	133,305.70	2630.83	2767.15	2371.24	2599.40	735.58	2494.00
Total	761,561.22	10,175.97	9909.09	8532.42	9831.39	3807.97	9715.32

Source IRDAI Handbook of Statistics (IRDAI, 2012, 2015)

Table 3.8   Growth of infrastructure investment (%)

Year	LICI	ICICI	BAJAJ	SBI	HDFC	BIRLA	MAX
2005–2006	7.89	42.17	91.72	70.66	148.58	32.23	46.95
2006–2007	40.33	36.39	72.89	51.04	17.62	77.27	82.53
2007–2008	−11.68	46.59	64.88	62.93	45.41	84.87	79.72
2008–2009	3.94	16.41	26.17	1.83	36.14	53.68	17.57
2009–2010	27.27	30.79	104.76	16.75	69.92	95.96	51.57
2010–2011	1.90	57.03	3.53	−3.70	54.27	29.24	47.84
2011–2012	5.02	55.99	49.19	48.01	25.73	51.33	57.30
2012–2013	20.66	43.42	25.42	26.55	24.54	0.69	20.95
2013–2014	30.69	8.80	36.69	69.59	27.52	−9.83	15.88
Average	471.29	37.51	52.80	38.18	49.97	46.16	46.70

Source Compilation on the basis of Table 3.7 using MS Excel 2007

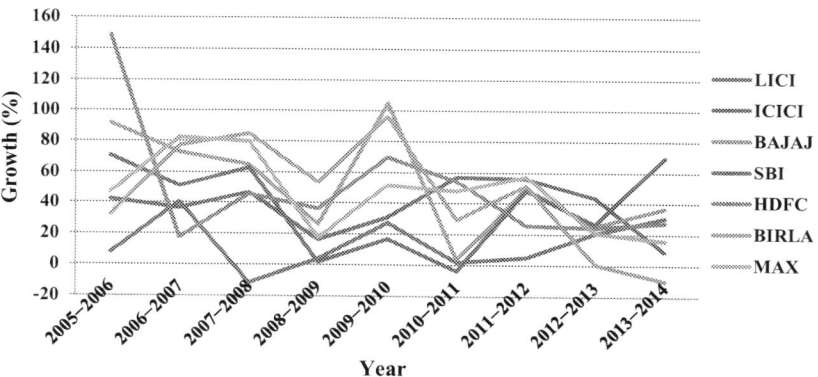

Chart 3.4   Growth of infrastructure investment (*Source* Compiled based on Table 3.8 using MS Excel)

Findings

- Growth of II for all the sample companies was really volatile during the study period. However, a common trend is observed among them. Growth of II for almost all the sample companies fell during

2007–2008 to 2008–2009 followed by a sudden rise in the following year. Currently, growth of II is showing an increasing trend for SBI, BAJAJ and LICI, while others are projecting a declining trend.

- In terms of average growth, LICI is an outlier with 471.29% growth. Among the private companies, BAJAJ is projecting highest average growth followed by HDFC. ICICI with 37.51% average growth is at the bottom.

Table 3.9 projects approved investments by select life insurance companies during the study period.

Growth of approved investments during the study period is shown in Table 3.10.

The result of Table 3.10 is projected in Chart 3.5.

Findings

- While all the companies are projecting a declining trend in terms of average growth of AI during the period, the AI of LICI grew significantly in the year 2008–2009 probably due to investors' increasing confidence in public sector in the post-scam era.
- In terms of average growth of AI, LICI is an outlier with 445% growth during the period. Among the private companies, MAX is projecting highest average growth followed by SBI. However, average growth of BIRLA is really less.

Other than approved investment by the select life insurance companies during the study period is shown in Table 3.11.

Growth analysis of other than approved investments of the seven life insurance companies is made in Table 3.12.

The result of the above table is shown in Chart 3.6.

Findings

- Growth of OAI for all the sample companies was very volatile during the study period. It showed an increasing trend in the years 2006–2007, 2009–2010 and 2011–2012 and showed a reverse trend in the others. Growth of HDFC during 2006–2007 was significantly higher than its peers in the sample.
- In terms of average growth, LICI with 1475.14% growth is outperforming all other companies. However, among the private players,

Table 3.9 Approved Investment (As on 31st March) (Rs. in Crores)

Year	LICI	ICICI	BAJAJ	SBI	HDFC	BIRLA	MAX
2004–2005	98,018.26	2123.99	389.99	153.03	403.17	1065.36	38.24
2005–2006	96,927.04	6667.22	2478.70	686.82	1667.11	1924.39	171.79
2006–2007	128,683.34	11,500.67	4445.10	2187.03	3498.54	3271.09	692.89
2007–2008	19,505.64	20,292.56	9646.32	5491.51	6546.03	5494.11	1554.17
2008–2009	267,138.60	27,114.52	13,333.24	8821.66	7651.97	7458.38	3082.60
2009–2010	393,001.30	48,473.37	27,749.85	21,170.96	16,019.69	13,090.88	6508.96
2010–2011	447,815.50	57,994.73	32,380.97	31,230.78	21,519.21	16,859.48	8158.95
2011–2012	486,498.90	59,932.67	31,165.91	35,136.92	25,381.61	17,594.39	10,485.69
2012–2013	527,660.36	60,054.26	27,347.64	34,779.47	30,691.28	18,819.43	11,863.81
2013–2014	553,985.23	64,202.56	24,542.35	39,757.79	38,684.94	20,447.05	12,836.00
Total	3,019,234.17	358,356.60	173,480.10	179,415.97	152,063.55	106,024.56	55,393.10

Source IRDAI Handbook of Statistics (IRDAI, 2012, 2015)

Table 3.10 Growth of approved investment (%)

Year	LICI	ICICI	BAJAJ	SBI	HDFC	BIRLA	MAX
2005–2006	−1.11	213.90	535.58	348.81	313.50	80.63	349.24
2006–2007	32.76	72.50	79.33	218.43	109.86	69.98	303.34
2007–2008	−84.84	76.45	117.01	151.09	87.11	67.96	124.30
2008–2009	1269.55	33.62	38.22	60.64	16.89	35.75	98.34
2009–2010	47.12	78.77	108.13	139.99	109.35	75.52	111.15
2010–2011	13.95	19.64	16.69	47.52	34.33	28.79	25.35
2011–2012	8.64	3.34	−3.75	12.51	17.95	4.36	28.52
2012–2013	8.46	0.20	−12.25	−1.02	20.92	6.96	13.14
2013–2014	4.99	6.91	−10.26	14.31	26.05	8.65	8.19
Average	445.00	56.15	96.52	110.25	81.77	42.07	117.95

Source Compilation on the basis of Table 3.9 using MS Excel 2007

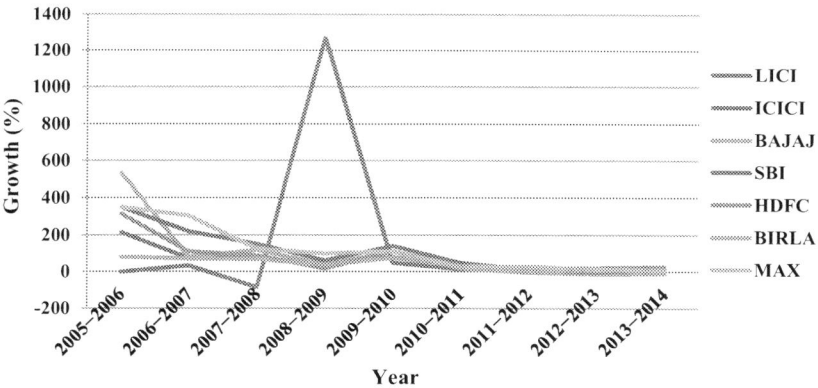

Chart 3.5 Growth of approved investment (*Source* Compiled based on Table 3.10 using MS Excel)

HDFC is at the top followed by MAX. Average growth of ICICI is really low as compared to other companies in the sample.

3.4.2 Trend Analysis

If the distribution of Y_t over the study period is nonlinear, in the exponential form, it can be represented as $Y_t = ab^t$ (Makridakis et al., 2005).

Table 3.11 Other than approved investment (As on 31st March) (Rs. in Crores)

Year	LICI	ICICI	BAJAJ	SBI	HDFC	BIRLA	MAX
2004–2005	26,322.78	516.71	53.99	88.54	30.17	87.94	15.39
2005–2006	27,444.65	724.00	274.59	185.76	36.68	242.38	28.85
2006–2007	35,508.60	1121.56	838.27	492.99	303.66	212.56	113.17
2007–2008	53,057.64	3840.18	1436.90	1253.17	611.60	864.75	533.45
2008–2009	63,206.07	2801.13	1589.02	1211.26	560.49	644.33	366.47
2009–2010	45,150.42	4684.25	1920.32	1209.53	1001.11	1426.86	659.96
2010–2011	56,806.37	4013.20	2532.54	1102.82	459.31	1070.94	441.72
2011–2012	57,191.76	3280.96	1796.27	1272.64	890.96	1008.23	729.97
2012–2013	53,819.49	3297.73	1664.56	1236.77	1484.91	1270.90	486.61
2013–2014	28,370.79	3211.16	1573.11	337.11	941.87	1428.40	487.00
Total	446,878.57	27,490.88	13,679.57	8390.59	6320.76	8257.29	3862.59

Source IRDAI Handbook of Statistics (IRDAI, 2012, 2015)

Table 3.12 Growth of other than approved investment (%)

Year	LICI	ICICI	BAJAJ	SBI	HDFC	BIRLA	MAX
2005–2006	4.26	40.12	408.59	109.80	21.58	175.62	87.46
2006–2007	29.38	54.91	205.28	165.39	727.86	−12.30	292.27
2007–2008	49.42	242.40	71.41	154.20	101.41	306.83	371.37
2008–2009	19.13	−27.06	10.59	−3.34	−8.36	−25.49	−31.30
2009–2010	−28.57	67.23	20.85	−0.14	78.61	121.45	80.09
2010–2011	25.82	−14.33	31.88	−8.82	−54.12	−24.94	−33.07
2011–2012	0.68	−18.25	−29.07	15.40	93.98	−5.86	65.26
2012–2013	−5.90	0.51	−7.33	−2.82	66.66	26.05	−33.34
2013–2014	−47.29	−2.63	−5.49	−72.74	−36.57	12.39	0.08
Average	1475.14	38.10	78.52	39.66	110.12	63.75	88.76

Source Compilation on the basis of Table 3.11 using MS Excel 2007

Therefore, the trend of a variable is analysed using exponential equation. The main objective here is to explore the increase or decrease in the value of a variable with respect to time. Here, the value of the variable is the dependent variable (DV) and time represented by year is the independent variable (IV). Now, this relationship is established to find out the Compound Annual Growth Rate (CAGR), based on the following equation:

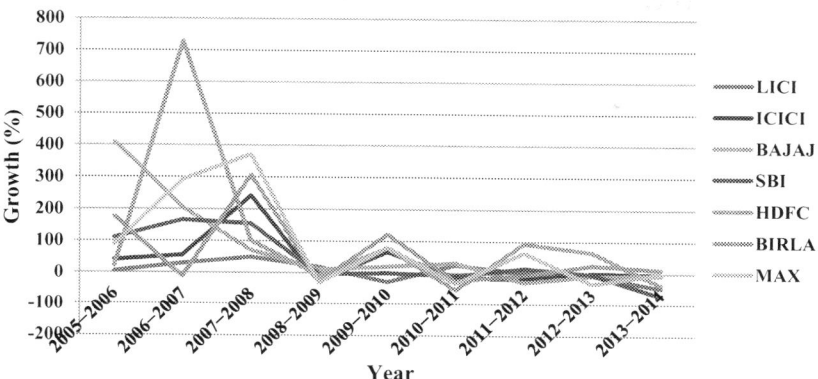

Chart 3.6 Growth of other than approved investment (*Source* Compiled based on Table 3.12 using MS Excel)

$$\text{CAGR } (g) = \left(\frac{\text{Ending Value}}{\text{Beginning Value}} \right)^{\frac{1}{\text{Number of Years}}} - 1$$

$$\Rightarrow (g+1)^t = \left(\frac{Y_t}{Y_1} \right)^{\frac{t}{t}}$$

$$\Rightarrow (g+1)^t = \frac{Y_t}{Y_1}$$

Now, the above expression is rewritten in the following Eq. (3.1)

$$\Rightarrow Y_t = Y_1 \times (1+g)^t \tag{3.1}$$

where

- Y_t = Value at time t;
- Y_1 = Value in the beginning year; and
- g = CAGR.

If $Y_1 = a$ and $(1 + g) = b$, the above equation represents an exponential trend in the following way:

$$\Rightarrow Y_t = ab^t \tag{3.2}$$

Therefore, a nonlinear relationship can be established between value of the variable and time period. It is statistically known as exponential relationship. In order to get the trend of Υ_t during the study period, the values of 'a' and 'b' are estimated. For this purpose, the above nonlinear equation is transformed into a linear equation by taking logarithm at both sides of equation. Now, the equation is:

$$\Rightarrow \text{Log } Y_t = \text{Log } a + t \text{ Log } b \qquad (3.3)$$

Then, the observed values of Υ_t are log transformed using SPSS 20.0 for calculation of the values of 'log a' and 'log b', and the values of log a and log b are estimated using simple least square regression. After measuring the values of log a and log b, the values of 'a' and 'b' are measured by taking antilog of 'log a' and 'log b' (Makridakis et al., 2005). Putting these values of 'a' and 'b' in Eq. (3.2), estimated trend values of Υ_t are calculated. In Eq. (3.2), 'b' is represented by $(1 + g)$ where 'g' is CAGR for the study period. From the estimated value of 'b', the value of the CAGR is calculated based on the following equation:

$$\Rightarrow \text{CAGR}(\%) = (b-1) \times 100 \qquad (3.4)$$

3.4.2.1   Trend of Premium Collection

In this segment, the trend of premium collection of the sample companies is analysed during the study period. Based on the observed values in Table 3.1, the estimated trends of total premium collection are calculated using the aforesaid methodology. Estimated values of 'log a', 'log b', 'a', 'b' and trend values of total premium during study period are presented in Table 3.13.

Trend lines fitted on the basis of trend values of premium collection during the study period are shown in Chart 3.7.

Findings

- All the companies in the sample are projecting an increasing trend during the study period.
- Among the private companies, ICICI is projecting highest trend of premium collection throughout the study period. However, in 2013–2014, the trend of premium collection for BAJAJ is more than that of ICICI. BIRLA on the other hand is projecting lowest trend in premium collection.

Table 3.13 Trend in total premium collection (As on 31st March) (Rs. in Crores)

Year	LICI	ICICI	BAJAJ	SBI	HDFC	BIRLA	MAX
2004–2005	90,762.376	4886.538	1256.138	3192.091	1327.801	1336.609	741.2121
2005–2006	102,232.02	5741.194	1722.165	3674.097	1775.271	1629.327	1004.342
2006–2007	115,151.08	6745.329	2361.088	4228.886	2373.537	1986.149	1360.884
2007–2008	129,702.72	7925.087	3237.051	4867.448	3173.419	2421.116	1843.998
2008–2009	146,093.25	9311.184	4437.997	5602.432	4242.861	2951.34	2498.617
2009–2010	164,555.06	10,939.71	6084.494	6448.399	5672.705	3597.683	3385.626
2010–2011	185,349.88	12,853.07	8341.842	7422.108	7584.406	4385.576	4587.523
2011–2012	208,772.54	15,101.07	11,436.67	8542.846	10,140.35	5346.017	6216.094
2012–2013	235,155.13	17,742.24	15,679.67	9832.816	13,557.65	6516.795	8422.807
2013–2014	264,871.68	20,845.36	21,496.82	11,317.57	18,126.58	7943.973	11,412.9
Log a	11.297	3.62	3.44	2.96	3.00	3.04	2.74
Log b	0.119	0.07	0.06	0.14	0.13	0.09	0.13
a	80,579.54	4159.11	2773.32	916.22	993.12	1096.48	547.02
b	1.12637	1.174	1.151	1.371	1.337	1.219	1.355
CAGR	12.63699	17.40	15.10	37.10	33.70	21.90	35.50

Source Table 3.1

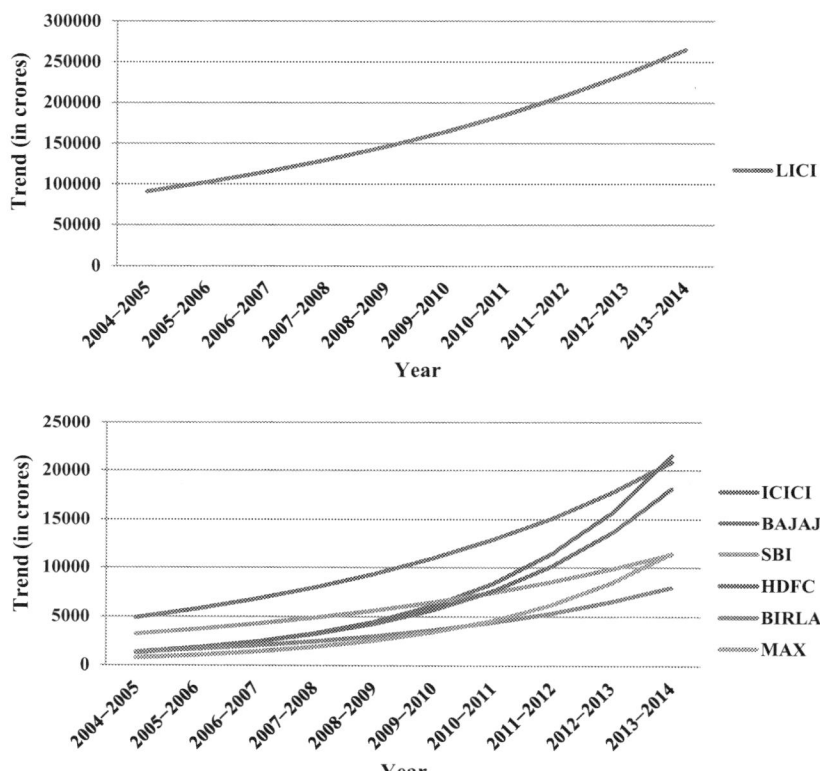

Chart 3.7   Trend of total premium collection (*Source* Table 3.13)

- CAGR is highest for SBI followed by MAX. It is lowest for LICI.

3.4.2.2   *Trend of Total Investment*
In this section, the trend of total investment is measured to explore the increase or decrease of the total investment of the sample companies during the study period (Table 3.14).

Trend values are plotted in Chart 3.8.

Table 3.14 Trend in total investment (As on 31st March) (Rs. in Crores)

Year	LICI	ICICI	BAJAJ	SBI	HDFC	BIRLA	MAX
2004–2005	406,362.1355	6498.56	1754.31	2327.52	1769.45	1954.11	724.64
2005–2006	473,543.9475	9091.49	2768.30	3465.67	2677.18	2722.08	1130.43
2006–2007	551,832.5911	12,719.00	4368.38	5160.38	4050.58	3791.86	1763.47
2007–2008	643,064.3032	17,793.88	6893.30	7683.81	6128.52	5282.06	2751.02
2008–2009	749,378.8963	24,893.63	10,877.63	11,441.19	9272.46	7357.91	4291.59
2009–2010	873,269.9473	34,826.20	17,164.90	17,035.94	14,029.23	10,249.57	6694.88
2010–2011	1,017,643.284	48,721.85	27,086.21	25,366.51	21,226.22	14,277.65	10,444.01
2011–2012	1,185,885.139	68,161.86	42,742.05	37,770.74	32,115.28	19,888.76	16,292.65
2012–2013	1,381,941.576	95,358.45	67,446.95	56,240.63	48,590.41	27,705.05	25,416.54
2013–2014	1,610,411.04	133,406.47	106,431.29	83,742.29	73,517.29	38,593.13	39,649.80
Log a	12.762	3.667	3.194	3.046	3.068	3.147	2.667
Log b	0.153	0.146	0.173	0.198	0.18	0.144	0.193
a	348,711.426	4645.15	1563.14	1111.73	1169.5	1402.81	464.51
b	1.16532498	1.399	1.489	1.578	1.513	1.393	1.56
CAGR	16.5324979	39.90	48.90	57.80	51.30	39.30	56.00

Source Table 3.3

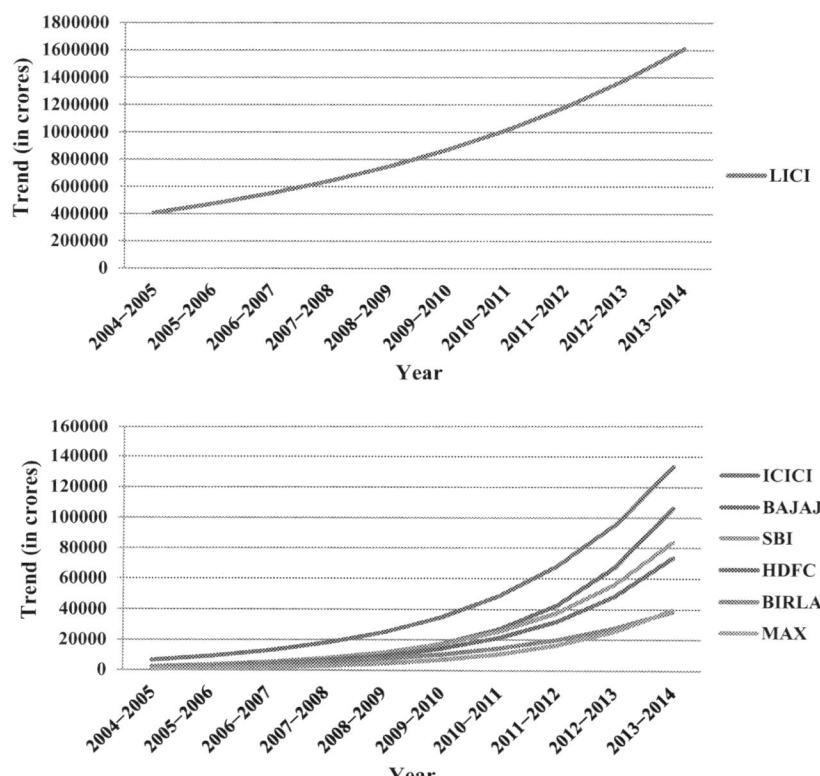

Chart 3.8   Trend of total investment (*Source* Table 3.14)

Findings

- All the companies are projecting an upward trend in terms of total investment. However, the trend of LICI is flatter as compared to other private companies.
- Trend of total investment is highest for ICICI followed by BAJAJ. However, it is least for BIRLA and MAX.
- In terms of CAGR, SBI is projecting highest growth rate followed by MAX, while it is least for the LICI.

3.4.2.3   Trend in Sectorial Investments

Analysis of trend of Investments in Government and Other Approved Securities (IGOAS), Infrastructure Investment (II), Approved Investment (AI) and Other than Approved Investment (OAI) is made using log-linear model. Initially, trend of IGOAS is analysed in Table 3.15 (Chart 3.9).

Findings

- All the companies are projecting an increasing trend. However, trend of LICI is flatter as compared to other private companies.
- The trend of IGOAS is highest for SBI among the private companies. It is followed by BAJAJ and ICICI. On the other hand, BIRLA is projecting a very low trend of IGOAS.
- In terms of CAGR, BAJAJ is at the top position followed by SBI. However, CAGR of the LICI is the least.

The trend of infrastructure investment of the sample companies during the study period is made as below (Table 3.16, Chart 3.10).

Table 3.15 Trend in investment in government and other approved securities (As on 31st March) (Rs. in Crores)

Year	LICI	ICICI	BAJAJ	SBI	HDFC	BIRLA	MAX
2004–2005	244,507.2	690.31	309.65	694.81	473.0821	100.74	360.664
2005–2006	281,250.3	929.16	461.07	1004.01	651.4341	144.56	514.307
2006–2007	323,514.9	1250.64	686.54	1450.79	897.0247	207.44	733.401
2007–2008	372,130.7	1683.37	1022.25	2096.39	1235.203	297.68	1045.830
2008–2009	428,052.3	2265.81	1522.14	3029.28	1700.875	427.17	1491.354
2009–2010	492,377.4	3049.78	2266.46	4377.31	2342.104	612.98	2126.671
2010–2011	566,369	4105.01	3374.76	6325.22	3225.078	879.63	3032.633
2011–2012	651,479.5	5525.34	5025.02	9139.94	4440.932	1262.27	4324.535
2012–2013	749,379.9	7437.11	7482.25	13,207.21	6115.163	1811.36	6166.786
2013–2014	861,992.2	10,010.35	11,141.07	19,084.42	8420.58	2599.30	8793.837
Log a	12.267	2.71	2.318	2.682	2.536	1.882	2.403
Log b	0.14	0.129	0.173	0.16	0.139	0.157	0.154
a	212,564.3	512.86	207.96	480.84	343.56	70.2	252.92
b	1.150274	1.346	1.489	1.445	1.377	1.435	1.426
CAGR	15.02738	34.60	48.90	44.50	37.70	43.50	42.60

Source Table 3.5

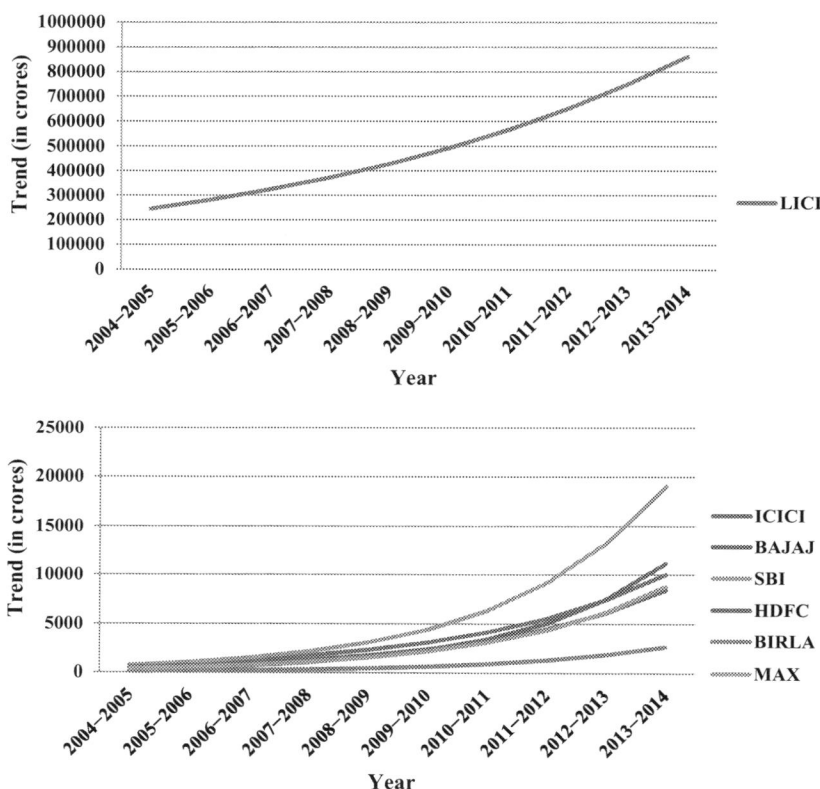

Chart 3.9 Trend in investment in government and other approved securities (*Source* Table 3.15)

Findings

- While all the companies are projecting an upward trend in terms of infrastructure investment, the trend of infrastructure investment of LICI is much flatter as compared to its private counterparts.
- The trend of infrastructure investment of BAJAJ, SBI and ICICI is highest among the private companies. However, the trend of investment of BIRLA is much below.

Table 3.16 Trend in infrastructure investment (As on 31st March) (Rs. in Crores)

Year	LICI	ICICI	BAJAJ	SBI	HDFC	BIRLA	MAX
2004–2005	45,071.28	159.17	102.82	210.33	119.38	37.14	105.95
2005–2006	50,061.16	219.65	151.76	270.91	172.15	55.29	155.32
2006–2007	55,603.48	303.12	224.00	348.93	248.24	82.33	227.70
2007–2008	61,759.4	418.31	330.62	449.42	357.96	122.60	333.81
2008–2009	68,596.84	577.27	487.99	578.85	516.18	182.54	489.36
2009–2010	76,191.27	796.63	720.28	745.56	744.34	271.81	717.40
2010–2011	84,626.48	1099.34	1063.13	960.28	1073.33	404.72	1051.71
2011–2012	93,995.56	1517.09	1569.19	1236.84	1547.75	602.63	1541.81
2012–2013	104,401.9	2093.59	2316.12	1593.05	2231.85	897.32	2260.29
2013–2014	115,960.3	2889.15	3418.59	2051.85	3218.33	1336.11	3313.58
Log a	10.611	2.062	1.843	2.213	1.918	1.397	1.859
Log b	0.105	0.14	0.169	0.11	0.159	0.173	0.166
A	40,578.76	115.34	69.66	163.3	82.79	24.94	72.27
B	1.110711	1.38	1.476	1.288	1.442	1.489	1.466
CAGR	11.07106	38.00	47.60	28.80	44.20	48.90	46.60

Source Table 3.7

- BIRLA has the highest CAGR during the period followed by BAJAJ. However, just like other parameters, CAGR of LICI is very low.

The trend of approved investment of the sample life insurance companies on the basis of Table 3.9 is set as (Table 3.17, Chart 3.11).

Findings

- Approved investments of all the sample companies are projecting an increasing trend during the study period.
- Among private companies, a highest trend is observed for ICICI followed by SBI. However, a lowest trend of approved investment is observed for BIRLA and MAX.
- MAX has the highest CAGR during the period followed by SBI. However, LICI is once again at the last position.

The trend of other than approved investments of the sample companies is placed as Table 3.18 (Chart 3.12).

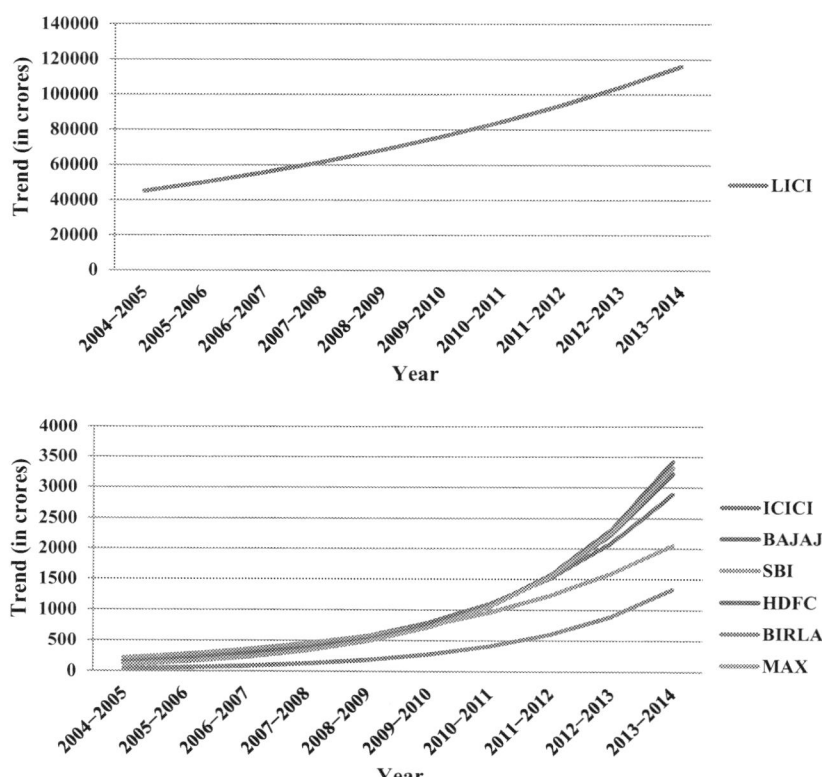

Chart 3.10   Trend in infrastructure investment (*Source* Table 3.16)

Findings

- Other than approved investments of the entire sample companies are projecting an upward trend during the study period. However, OAI of LICI is almost projecting a linear trend during the period contrary to the trend behaviour of other private companies.
- Among the sample private companies, trend of ICICI is at the highest position followed by BAJAJ. However, trend projection for MAX is really low.

Table 3.17 Trend in approved investment (As on 31st March) (Rs. in Crores)

Year	LICI	ICICI	BAJAJ	SBI	HDFC	BIRLA	MAX
2004–2005	63,133.07	4885.39	1563.06	502.29	1027.86	1625.37	133.94
2005–2006	82,371.93	6947.03	2360.22	907.64	1625.04	2264.14	247.66
2006–2007	107,473.5	9878.68	3563.94	1640.11	2569.19	3153.94	457.92
2007–2008	140,224.5	14,047.48	5381.54	2963.67	4061.89	4393.44	846.69
2008–2009	182,955.8	19,975.52	8126.13	5355.36	6421.84	6120.06	1565.54
2009–2010	238,708.8	28,405.19	12,270.46	9677.14	10,152.93	8525.24	2894.68
2010–2011	311,451.8	40,392.18	18,528.39	17,486.58	16,051.78	11,875.67	5352.26
2011–2012	406,362	57,437.67	27,977.87	31,598.26	25,377.87	16,542.80	9896.32
2012–2013	530,194.8	81,676.37	42,246.59	57,098.05	40,122.41	23,044.12	18,298.30
2013–2014	691,763.7	116,143.80	63,792.34	103,176.18	63,433.53	32,100.46	33,833.55
Log a	10.787	3.536	3.015	2.444	2.813	3.067	1.86
Log b	0.266	0.153	0.179	0.257	0.199	0.144	0.267
a	48,387.66	3435.58	1035.14	277.97	650.13	1166.81	72.44
b	1.304735	1.422	1.51	1.807	1.581	1.393	1.849
CAGR	30.47351	42.20	51.00	80.70	58.10	39.30	84.90

Source Table 3.9

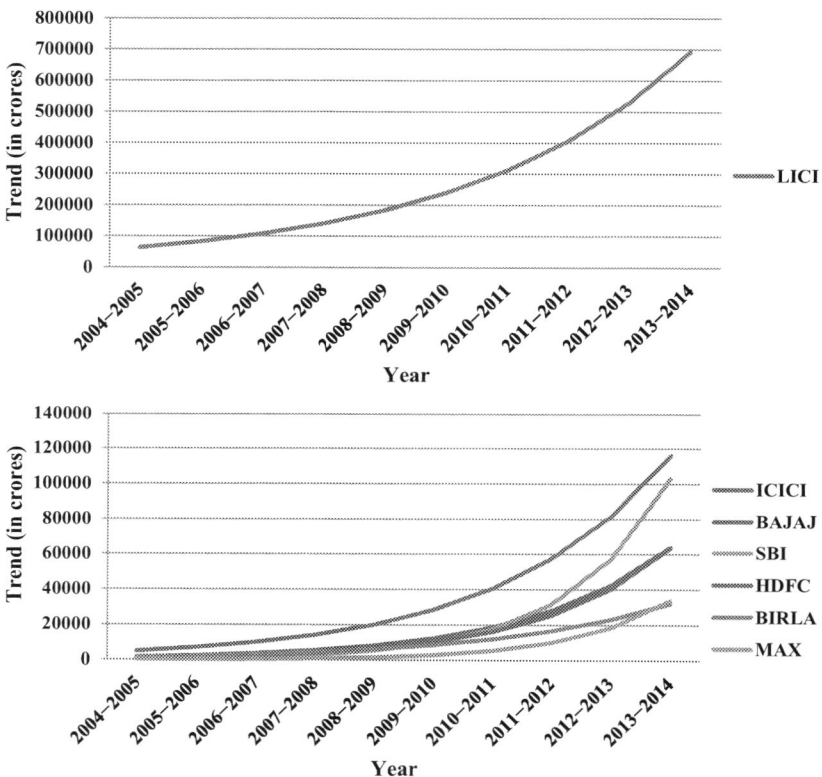

Chart 3.11   Trend in approved investment (*Source* Table 3.17)

- In terms of CAGR, HDFC is at the highest position followed by MAX. LICI is projecting the least CAGR in other than approved investments.

3.4.3   Correlation Analysis

3.4.3.1   Correlation Between Total Premium and Total Investment
Total investment of the life insurance companies comes from different sources. Premium collection is one of those sources, and there is a relationship between premium collection and total investment. In this

Table 3.18   Trend in other than approved investments (As on 31st March) (Rs. in Crores)

Year	LICI	ICICI	BAJAJ	SBI	HDFC	BIRLA	MAX
2004–2005	34,509.83	900.98	253.95	278.03	70.45	174.15	44.98
2005–2006	36,134.35	1100.09	340.80	332.80	102.51	230.05	64.86
2006–2007	37,835.34	1343.21	457.35	398.36	149.15	303.89	93.52
2007–2008	39,616.4	1640.06	613.76	476.84	217.01	401.44	134.86
2008–2009	41,481.3	2002.52	823.67	570.77	315.75	530.31	194.47
2009–2010	43,433.99	2445.07	1105.36	683.22	459.41	700.54	280.42
2010–2011	45,478.6	2985.43	1483.40	817.81	668.45	925.41	404.36
2011–2012	47,619.46	3645.21	1990.72	978.92	972.59	1222.47	583.09
2012–2013	49,861.1	4450.80	2671.55	1171.76	1415.11	1614.88	840.82
2013–2014	52,208.26	5434.43	3585.21	1402.60	2058.99	2133.25	1212.46
Log a	10.403	2.868	2.277	2.366	1.685	2.12	1.494
Log b	0.046	0.087	0.128	0.078	0.163	0.121	0.159
a	32,958.35	737.9	189.23	232.27	48.42	131.83	31.19
b	1.047074	1.221	1.342	1.197	1.455	1.321	1.442
CAGR	4.707441	22.10	34.20	19.70	45.50	32.10	44.20

Source Table 3.11

segment, the relationship between premium collection and total invest-ment is measured during the study period on the basis of original data set of Tables 3.1 and 3.3 using the Pearson's correlation coefficient (r). It measures the strength of association between two variables. It is denoted by r that ranges within ± 1. If $r = 0$, it indicates no association between two variables. However, $r < 0$ indicates negative correlation and $r > 0$ indicates positive correlation (Das, 1990). Statistical significance of the 'r' is also tested using t-test based on the following hypothesis:

- *Null Hypothesis (H_0): There is no significant correlation between premium collection and total investment.*
- *Alternate Hypothesis (H_1): There is significant correlation between premium collection and total investment.*

At 5% level of significance, if probability of accepting the test statistic in t-distribution table is less than 0.05, H_0 is not accepted and vice versa. The Pearson's correlation coefficient between premium collection and total investment for the sample companies and their statistical significance based on the original data during the study period is shown in Table 3.19.

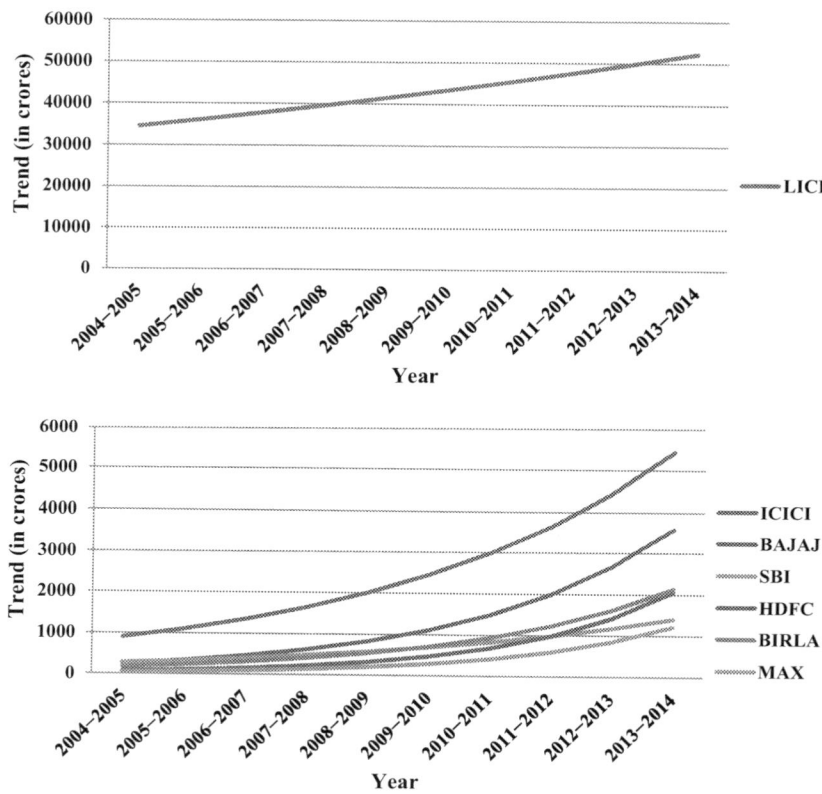

Chart 3.12   Trend in other than approved investments (*Source* Table 3.18)

Findings

- A positive relationship between premium collection and total investments is observed for all the companies under consideration.
- The correlation between premium collection and total investment is also statistically significant for all the companies except for BAJAJ.
- While correlation coefficient for LICI, HDFC and MAX is really high, it is moderate for SBI, BIRLA and ICICI.

Table 3.19 Correlation between premium collection and total investment

Life insurance companies	Pearson's correlation coefficient (r)	P-Value	Decision rule	Decision based on H_0
LICI	0.950	0.000	p-value < 0.05	H_0 is rejected
ICICI	0.751	0.012	p-value < 0.05	H_0 is rejected
BAJAJ	0.535	0.111	p-value > 0.05	H_0 is accepted
SBI	0.893	0.001	p-value < 0.05	H_0 is rejected
HDFC	0.968	0.000	p-value < 0.05	H_0 is rejected
BIRLA	0.887	0.001	p-value < 0.05	H_0 is rejected
MAX	0.957	0.000	p-value < 0.05	H_0 is rejected

Source Tables 3.1 and 3.3

3.4.3.2 Correlation Among Life Insurance Companies
Correlation among the life insurance companies in terms of premium collection, total investments and other sectorial investments, such as IGOAS, II, AI and OAI is discussed in the current segment.

a. Premium Collection

Correlation coefficients (r) among the premium collection of select life insurance companies during the study period along with their statistical significance based on the methodology described above are shown in Table 3.20.

Findings

- Premium collection of all the companies under consideration is positively correlated.
- While this correlation is significant for most of the companies, premium collection of BAJAJ is not significantly correlated with that of LICI, HDFC and MAX.

b. Total Investment

The correlation coefficients among the companies along with their statistical significance in terms of total investments of the companies are shown in Table 3.21.

Table 3.20 Correlation among life insurance companies in terms of premium collection

		LICI	ICICI	BAJAJ	SBI	HDFC	BIRLA	MAX
LICI	Pearson Correlation	1	0.813	**0.583**	0.941	0.977	0.915	0.982
	Sig. (2-tailed)		0.004	**0.077**	0.000	0.000	0.000	0.000
ICICI	Pearson Correlation	0.813	1	0.930	0.867	0.721	0.920	0.770
	Sig. (2-tailed)	0.004		0.000	0.001	0.019	0.000	0.009
BAJAJ	Pearson Correlation	**0.583**	0.930	1	0.643	**0.451**	0.750[*]	**0.513**
	Sig. (2-tailed)	**0.077**	0.000		0.045	**0.191**	0.013	**0.129**
SBI	Pearson Correlation	0.941	0.867	0.643[*]	1	0.923	0.978	0.952
	Sig. (2-tailed)	0.000	0.001	0.045		0.000	0.000	0.000
HDFC	Pearson Correlation	0.977	0.721[*]	0.451	0.923	1	0.886	0.993
	Sig. (2-tailed)	0.000	0.019	0.191	0.000		0.001	0.000
BIRLA	Pearson Correlation	0.915	0.920	0.750[*]	0.978	0.886	1	0.928
	Sig. (2-tailed)	0.000	0.000	0.013	0.000	0.001		0.000
MAX	Pearson Correlation	0.982	0.770	0.513	0.952	0.993	0.928	1
	Sig. (2-tailed)	0.000	0.009	0.129	0.000	0.000	0.000	

Source Table 3.1

Findings

- Total investments of all the select companies have significant positive correlation among them.

c. Investment in Government and Other Approved Securities

Table 3.21 Correlation among life insurance companies in terms of total investments

		LICI	ICICI	BAJAJ	SBI	HDFC	BIRLA	MAX
LICI	Pearson Correlation	1	0.972	0.935	0.992	0.992	0.985	0.995
	Sig. (2-tailed)		0.000	0.000	0.000	0.000	0.000	0.000
ICICI	Pearson Correlation	0.972	1	0.991	0.981	0.950	0.997	0.959
	Sig. (2-tailed)	0.000		0.000	0.000	0.000	0.000	0.000
BAJAJ	Pearson Correlation	0.935	0.991	1	0.954	0.904	0.981	0.918
	Sig. (2-tailed)	0.000	0.000		0.000	0.000	0.000	0.000
SBI	Pearson Correlation	0.992	0.981	0.954	1	0.987	0.993	0.994
	Sig. (2-tailed)	0.000	0.000	0.000		0.000	0.000	0.000
HDFC	Pearson Correlation	0.992	0.950	0.904	0.987	1	0.969	0.998
	Sig. (2-tailed)	0.000	0.000	0.000	0.000		0.000	0.000
BIRLA	Pearson Correlation	0.985	0.997	0.981	0.993	0.969	1	0.978
	Sig. (2-tailed)	0.000	0.000	0.000	0.000	0.000		0.000
MAX	Pearson Correlation	0.995	0.959	0.918	0.994	0.998	0.978	1
	Sig. (2-tailed)	0.000	0.000	0.000	0.000	0.000	0.000	

Source Table 3.3

Correlation among select life insurance companies in terms of their investment in Government and other approved securities along with their statistical significance is shown in Table 3.22.

Findings

- Positive significant relationship exists among the sample life insurance companies in terms of investment in Government and other approved securities.

d. Infrastructure Investment

The correlation coefficient among infrastructure investments of the sample life insurance companies and their statistical significance during the study period is shown in Table 3.23.

Table 3.22 Correlation among life insurance companies in terms of investments in IGOAS

		LICI	ICICI	BAJAJ	SBI	HDFC	BIRLA	MAX
LICI	Pearson Correlation	1	0.991	0.991	0.993	0.994	0.973	0.990
	Sig. (2-tailed)		0.000	0.000	0.000	0.000	0.000	0.000
ICICI	Pearson Correlation	0.991	1	0.993	0.998	0.995	0.981	0.990
	Sig. (2-tailed)	0.000		0.000	0.000	0.000	0.000	0.000
BAJAJ	Pearson Correlation	0.991	0.993	1	0.994	0.999	0.964	0.998
	Sig. (2-tailed)	0.000	0.000		0.000	0.000	0.000	0.000
SBI	Pearson Correlation	0.993	0.998	0.994	1	0.996	0.984	0.990
	Sig. (2-tailed)	0.000	0.000	0.000		0.000	0.000	0.000
HDFC	Pearson Correlation	0.994	0.995	0.999	0.996	1	0.972	0.997
	Sig. (2-tailed)	0.000	0.000	0.000	0.000		0.000	0.000
BIRLA	Pearson Correlation	0.973	0.981	0.964	0.984	0.972	1	0.957
	Sig. (2-tailed)	0.000	0.000	0.000	0.000	0.000		0.000
MAX	Pearson Correlation	0.990	0.990	0.998	0.990	0.997	0.957	1
	Sig. (2-tailed)	0.000	0.000	0.000	0.000	0.000	0.000	

Source Table 3.5

Table 3.23 Correlation among select life insurance companies in terms of II

		LICI	ICICI	BAJAJ	SBI	HDFC	BIRLA	MAX
LICI	Pearson Correlation	1	0.935	0.972	0.970	0.957	0.845	0.939
	Sig. (2-tailed)		0.000	0.000	0.000	0.000	0.002	0.000
ICICI	Pearson Correlation	0.935	1	0.979	0.932	0.986	0.927	0.994
	Sig. (2-tailed)	0.000		0.000	0.000	0.000	0.000	0.000
BAJAJ	Pearson Correlation	0.972	0.979	1	0.966	0.992	0.923	0.987
	Sig. (2-tailed)	0.000	0.000		0.000	0.000	0.000	0.000
SBI	Pearson Correlation	0.970	0.932	0.966	1	0.942	0.808	0.933
	Sig. (2-tailed)	0.000	0.000	0.000		0.000	0.005	0.000
HDFC	Pearson Correlation	0.957	0.986	0.992	0.942	1	0.942	0.994
	Sig. (2-tailed)	0.000	0.000	0.000	0.000		0.000	0.000
BIRLA	Pearson Correlation	0.845	0.927	0.923	0.808	0.942	1	0.955
	Sig. (2-tailed)	0.002	0.000	0.000	0.005	0.000		0.000
MAX	Pearson Correlation	0.939	0.994	0.987	0.933	0.994	0.955	1
	Sig. (2-tailed)	0.000	0.000	0.000	0.000	0.000	0.000	

Source Table 3.7

Findings

- Infrastructure investments of the select life insurance companies are significantly positively correlated.

e. Approved Investments

Significant correlation among approved investments made by the select life insurance companies is analysed with the help of Table 3.24.

Table 3.24 Correlation among select life insurance companies in terms of AI

		LICI	ICICI	BAJAJ	SBI	HDFC	BIRLA	MAX
LICI	Pearson Correlation	1	0.953	0.903	0.962	0.932	0.961	0.964
	Sig. (2-tailed)		0.000	0.000	0.000	0.000	0.000	0.000
ICICI	Pearson Correlation	0.953	1	0.968	0.983	0.946	0.995	0.970
	Sig. (2-tailed)	0.000		0.000	0.000	0.000	0.000	0.000
BAJAJ	Pearson Correlation	0.903	0.968	1	0.924	0.837	0.941	0.890
	Sig. (2-tailed)	0.000	0.000		0.000	0.003	0.000	0.001
SBI	Pearson Correlation	0.962	0.983	0.924	1	0.975	0.994	0.991
	Sig. (2-tailed)	0.000	0.000	0.000		0.000	0.000	0.000
HDFC	Pearson Correlation	0.932	0.946	0.837	0.975	1	0.972	0.988
	Sig. (2-tailed)	0.000	0.000	0.003	0.000		0.000	0.000
BIRLA	Pearson Correlation	0.961	0.995	0.941	0.994	0.972	1	0.988
	Sig. (2-tailed)	0.000	0.000	0.000	0.000	0.000		0.000
MAX	Pearson Correlation	0.964	0.970	0.890	0.991	0.988	0.988	1
	Sig. (2-tailed)	0.000	0.000	0.001	0.000	0.000	0.000	

Source Table 3.9

Findings

- In terms of approved investments too, the sample life insurance companies are significantly positively correlated.

f. Other than Approved Investment

Correlation coefficients along with their statistical significance among the sample life insurance companies in terms of other than approved investments are shown in Table 3.25.

Findings

- Infrastructure investments of all the sample life insurance companies are positively correlated.
- OAI of LICI is not significantly correlated with that of HDFC and BIRLA.
- OAI of SBI is not significantly correlated with that of BIRLA.

3.5   CONCLUSION

The chapter makes an attempt to analyse the growth of premium collection, total investment and sectorial investments of LICI and select other private life insurance companies during the post-reforms period. Total investments of life insurers are invested in four specific sectors in the proportion—investment in Government and other approved securities, infrastructure investments, approved investments and other than approved investments prescribed by the IRDAI. It has been observed that the LICI has been continuously losing its market share from the private peers in terms of premium collection and total investment. Among the private players considered in the study, the SBI has secured the top position while BIRLA was among the least performers. Growth of sectorial investments during the study period was volatile and it reached to its minimum during global economic recession. During recession, investment in Government and other approved securities has shown a sudden surge as compared to other sectors. At the same time, growth in sectorial investments by LICI was significantly higher from its private players

Table 3.25 Correlation among select life insurance companies in terms of OAI

		LICI	ICICI	BAJAJ	SBI	HDFC	BIRLA	MAX
LICI	Pearson Correlation	1	0.657	0.741	0.939	0.463	0.404	0.645
	Sig. (2-tailed)		0.039	0.014	0.000	0.178	0.246	0.044
ICICI	Pearson Correlation	0.657	1	0.913	0.814	0.717	0.897	0.916
	Sig. (2-tailed)	0.039		0.000	0.004	0.020	0.000	0.000
BAJAJ	Pearson Correlation	0.741	0.913	1	0.793	0.646	0.819	0.829
	Sig. (2-tailed)	0.014	0.000		0.006	0.044	0.004	0.003
SBI	Pearson Correlation	0.939	0.814	0.793	1	0.638	0.590	0.806
	Sig. (2-tailed)	0.000	0.004	0.006		0.047	0.073	0.005
HDFC	Pearson Correlation	0.463	0.717	0.646	0.638	1	0.861	0.787
	Sig. (2-tailed)	0.178	0.020	0.044	0.047		0.001	0.007
BIRLA	Pearson Correlation	0.404	0.897	0.819	0.590	0.861	1	0.870
	Sig. (2-tailed)	0.246	0.000	0.004	0.073	0.001		0.001
MAX	Pearson Correlation	0.645	0.916	0.829	0.806	0.787	0.870	1
	Sig. (2-tailed)	0.044	0.000	0.003	0.005	0.007	0.001	

Source Table 3.11

during this tenure. Hence, in terms of average growth in sectorial investments, LICI has outperformed its private peers. However, among the private players, SBI, BAJAJ and HDFC were the front runners while ICICI lagged behind other private insurers considered for the study.

In the following segment, an endeavour has been made to identify the trend of premium collection, total investments and sectorial investments during the study period using log-linear model. It has been observed that companies under consideration are projecting an increasing trend in terms of all the identified parameters. However, LICI's progress over the years is slow-paced as compared to its private peers. Among the private players, ICICI is projecting a promising trend for most of the parameters. However, SBI and BAJAJ are also not far behind. On the other hand, BIRLA is not depicting potential for growth among the private players. However, in terms of CAGR of infrastructure investments or approved investments, rather low-trending companies like BIRLA and MAX reported highest figures. However, in other parameters, SBI, BAJAJ and HDFC have secured the highest position. However, LICI has recorded the lowest CAGR for all the parameters.

In the final segment of the chapter, an analysis has been made to find out the correlation between premium collection and total investments during the study period for the sample companies using Pearson's correlation coefficient. It is evident that premium collection and total investments are positively and significantly correlated for all the companies except for BAJAJ. It is also observed that all the companies have significant positive correlation among themselves in terms of premium collection, total investments and other sectorial investments. However, premium collection of BAJAJ is not significantly correlated with that of LICI, HDFC and MAX. On the other hand, LICI is not significantly correlated with HDFC and BIRLA and SBI is not significantly correlated with BIRLA in terms of other than approved investments.

In the following chapter, the divergence among the LICI and select PLICs in terms of their premium collection, total investment and sectorial investments has been empirically analysed, and based on their relative nearness, a few homogenous groups have been formed out of them. Impact of global economic recession on select parameters, significant difference between public and private sector companies and impact of the select companies on industry performance have been empirically analysed in the following chapter.

References

Das, N. G. (1990). *Statistical methods in commerce, accountancy & economics (part-1)*. M. Das & Company.

IRDAI. (2012). *Handbook on Indian Insurance Statistics, 2011–2012*.

IRDAI. (2015). *Handbook on Indian Insurance Statistics, 2014–2015*.

Makridakis, S. C., Wheelwright, S., & Hyndman, R. J. (2005). *Forecasting methods and applications*. Wiley.

CHAPTER 4

An Empirical Insight into the Premium Mobilisation and Investment Portfolio of the LICI and Select Private Life Insurance Companies in India

Abstract Divergence among LICI and six select PLICs in term of their premium mobilisation, total investment and sectorial investments in the post-reform era has been analysed in this chapter. It is observed that the companies under consideration are significantly different from each another for these select parameters. LICI being the market leader projected an extra-ordinary performance in almost all the parameters. Impact of global economic recession on the select parameters has also been analysed in the following segment. Global economic recession in 2008–2009 significantly influenced the performances of those seven companies. Significant difference between public and private sector in terms of select parameters and impact of the sample companies on industry performance has also been analysed in this chapter. Ownership structure also has a significant impact on the performance of the companies for all the select parameters. When the performance of the individual companies was compared with the industry standards, it is observed that LICI significantly influences premium collection, IGOAS, II and OTAI of the industry, while ICICI has significant influence on the total investment of the industry.

© The Author(s), under exclusive license to Springer Nature
Singapore Pte Ltd. 2022
S. P. Patra et al., *Investment Pattern of LICI and Select Private LICs
in the Post-reforms Era in India*,
https://doi.org/10.1007/978-981-19-2799-7_4

Keywords One-way ANOVA · K-W test · Tukey HSD test · t test · M-W test · Regression · Global economic recession · Life insurance industry

4.1   INTRODUCTION

In the previous chapter, Chapter 3, an attempt has been made to analyse the growth and trend of premium mobilisation, total investment and sectorial investments of the LICI and select six private life insurance companies (PLICs) in the post-reforms era. An attempt has also been made to find out the correlation between premium collection and total investment during the study period for the sample companies. In this chapter, an attempt has been made to empirically analyse the divergence among the LICI and select PLICs in terms of their premium collection, total investment and sectorial investments and form a few homogenous groups among them based on their relative nearness. Impact of global economic recession on the select parameters has also been analysed in the following segment. Significant difference between public and private sector in terms of select parameters and impact of the sample companies on industry performance is finally analysed here.

4.2   OBJECTIVES OF THE STUDY

The objectives of the current chapter are:

a. To explore the significant difference among the LICI and six PLICs in terms of premium collection, total investment and four sectorial investments (Refer to Sect. 4.4.1);
b. To group the sample companies into homogenous subsets based on significant divergence among them in terms of premium collection, total investment and four sectorial investments (Refer to Sect. 4.4.2);
c. To study the impact of global economic recession on premium collection, total investment and four sectorial investments of the LICI and six PLICs (Refer to Sect. 4.4.3);

d. To examine the impact of ownership structure on premium collection, total investment and four sectorial investments of the LICI and six PLICs (Refer to Sect. 4.4.4);

e. To analyse the impact of the LICI and six PLICs on the entire life insurance sector in terms of premium collection, total investment and four sectorial investments (Refer to Sect. 4.4.5).

4.3 RESEARCH METHODS

The sampling design and collection of data for the current chapter is same as that of Chapter 3. The specific statistical tools used to fulfil the empirical objectives are highlighted here:

Sl. No	Objectives	Statistical Tools used
(a)	To explore the significant difference among the LICI and six PLICs in terms of premium collection, total investment and four sectorial investments;	• One-way Analysis of Variance (ANOVA) if the assumptions of normality and Homoscedasticity are fulfilled • Welch's test if the assumption of normality is fulfilled, but the assumption of Homoscedasticity is not fulfilled • Kruskal–Wallis (K-W) tests if both the assumptions are not fulfilled
(b)	To group the sample companies into homogenous subsets based on significant divergence among them in terms of premium collection, total investment and four sectorial investments;	• Tukey's Honestly Significant Difference (HSD) test as a post hoc test when the assumptions of normality and Homoscedasticity are fulfilled • Games-Howell test when the assumption is fulfilled but the assumption of Homoscedasticity is not fulfilled • Dunn-Bonferroni test as a post hoc test when both the assumptions are not fulfilled
(c)	To study the impact of global economic recession on premium collection, total investment and four sectorial investments of the LICI and six PLICs;	• Independent sample t-test if the assumption of normality is fulfilled • Mann-Whitney (M-W) test if the assumption of normality is not fulfilled

(continued)

(continued)

Sl. No	Objectives	Statistical Tools used
(d)	To examine the impact of ownership structure on premium collection, total investment and four sectorial investments of the LICI and six PLICs;	• Independent sample t-test if the assumption of normality is fulfilled • Mann-Whitney (M-W) test if the assumption of normality is not fulfilled
(e)	To analyse the impact of the LICI and six PLICs on the entire life insurance sector in terms of premium collection, total investment and four sectorial investments	• Multiple Linear Regression Analysis (a) Calculation of parameter estimates (β); (b) t-test (to measure significance of parameter estimates); (c) Calculation of Adjusted R^2 (strength of association); (d) F-test (model fitness)

4.4   ANALYSIS AND DISCUSSION

Based on the methodology adopted (refer to Sect. 4.3), the analysis of the collected data is divided into following segments.

4.4.1   Exploring Significant Difference Among Select Life Insurance Companies

With a view to analysing significant difference among select life insurers for Premium Collection (PC), Total Investment (TI) and four sectorial investments [Investment in Government and Other Approved Securities (IGOAS); Infrastructure Investments (II); Approved Investments (AI); and Other than Approved Investments (OAI)], one-way ANOVA is conducted subject to fulfilment of certain assumptions.

4.4.1.1   Assumptions

In the current segment, PC, TI, IGOAS, II, AI and OAI are considered as dependent variables (DVs) and the LICI and six PLICs are the independent variables (IVs). The DVs are measured at ratio scale. There are seven categorical groups, which are independent of one another. Two major assumptions for conducting one-way ANOVA are as follows:

(a) DVs should be approximately normally distributed across independent groups

The assumption is tested based on following hypothesis:

Hypothesis

- Null Hypothesis (H_0): DVs are approximately normally distributed across IVs;
- Alternate Hypothesis (H_1): DVs are not approximately normally distributed across IVs.

In order to test the aforesaid hypothesis, Shapiro-Wilks (S-W) test is conducted based on the following test statistic (W):

$$W = \frac{\left(\sum_{i=1}^{n} a i x(i)\right)^2}{\sum_{i=1}^{n} (xi - \bar{x})^2}$$

where

$X_{(i)}$ is the ith smallest number in the sample;
$a_i = m^T V^{-1}/C$ where
$m = (m_1, ..., m_n)^T$ (expected values of the order statistics and identically distributed random variables)
V = covariance matrix of the order statistics
$C = (m^T V^{-1} V^{-1} m)^{1/2}$

At 'n' degrees of freedom (DF) (where n = number of observations) and 5% level of significance, if the probability of obtaining the test statistics in normal distribution table is less than 0.05, H_0 cannot be accepted and vice versa. Results of S-W test are shown in Table 4.1.

The assumption is fulfilled for PC, IGOAS and AI. Hence, for these three variables, significant difference among select companies is to be tested using one-way ANOVA subject to fulfilment for the following assumption of Homoscedasticity. However, the assumption is not fulfilled for TI, II and OAI. Hence, the proposed test is K-W test for them.

Table 4.1 Results of S-W test

DV	IV	W	P-value	Decision rule	Decision based on H_0	Remarks
PC	BAJAJ	0.954	0.715	P-value > 0.05	H_0 is accepted	PC is approximately normally distributed across the companies. Assumption is fulfilled. **Proposed test: one-way ANOVA**
	BIRLA	0.855	0.067	P-value > 0.05	H_0 is accepted	
	HDFC	0.944	0.601	P-value > 0.05	H_0 is accepted	
	ICICI	0.888	0.160	P-value > 0.05	H_0 is accepted	
	LICI	0.941	0.569	P-value > 0.05	H0 is accepted	
	MAX	0.918	0.343	P-value > 0.05	H_0 is accepted	
	SBI	0.905	0.248	P-value > 0.05	H_0 is accepted	
TI	*BAJAJ*	*0.829*	*0.032*	*P-value < 0.05*	*H_0 is rejected*	TI is **not** approximately normally distributed across all the companies. The assumption is **not** fulfilled. **Proposed test: K-W test**
	BIRLA	0.893	0.185	P-value > 0.05	H_0 is accepted	
	HDFC	0.918	0.341	P-value > 0.05	H_0 is accepted	
	ICICI	0.886	0.155	P-value > 0.05	H_0 is accepted	
	LICI	0.945	0.604	P-value > 0.05	H_0 is accepted	
	MAX	0.907	0.259	P-value > 0.05	H_0 is accepted	
	SBI	0.890	0.172	P-value > 0.05	H_0 is accepted	
IGOAS	BAJAJ	0.874	0.110	P-value > 0.05	H_0 is accepted	IGOAS is approximately normally distributed across the companies. Assumption is fulfilled. **Proposed test: one-way ANOVA**
	BIRLA	0.877	0.122	P-value > 0.05	H_0 is accepted	
	HDFC	0.887	0.156	P-value > 0.05	H_0 is accepted	
	ICICI	0.893	0.181	P-value > 0.05	H_0 is accepted	
	LICI	0.928	0.431	P-value > 0.05	H_0 is accepted	
	MAX	0.859	0.074	P-value > 0.05	H_0 is accepted	
	SBI	0.902	0.229	P-value > 0.05	H_0 is accepted	
II	BAJAJ	0.898	0.206	P-value > 0.05	H_0 is accepted	TI is **not** approximately normally distributed across all the companies. The assumption is **not** fulfilled. **Proposed test: K-W test**
	BIRLA	0.861	0.079	P-value > 0.05	H_0 is accepted	

DV	IV	W	P-value	Decision rule	Decision based on H_0	Remarks
	HDFC	0.893	0.181	P-value > 0.05	H_0 is accepted	
	ICICI	*0.840*	*0.044*	*P-value < 0.05*	*H_0 is rejected*	
	LICI	0.924	0.395	P-value > 0.05	H_0 is accepted	
	MAX	0.877	0.120	P-value > 0.05	H_0 is accepted	
	SBI	0.866	0.090	P-value > 0.05	H_0 is accepted	AI is approximately normally distributed
AI	BAJAJ	0.878	0.125	P-value > 0.05	H_0 is accepted	across the companies. Assumption is
	BIRLA	0.887	0.158	P-value > 0.05	H_0 is accepted	fulfilled. **Proposed test: one-way**
	HDFC	0.917	0.330	P-value > 0.05	H_0 is accepted	**ANOVA**
	ICICI	0.864	0.084	P-value > 0.05	H_0 is accepted	
	LICI	0.890	0.168	P-value > 0.05	H_0 is accepted	
	MAX	0.881	0.135	P-value > 0.05	H_0 is accepted	
	SBI	0.853	0.063	P-value > 0.05	H_0 is accepted	
OAI	BAJAJ	0.923	0.383	P-value > 0.05	H_0 is accepted	TI is **not** approximately normally
	BIRLA	0.906	0.255	P-value > 0.05	H_0 is accepted	distributed across all the companies. The
	HDFC	0.957	0.752	P-value > 0.05	H_0 is accepted	assumption is **not** fulfilled. **Proposed**
	ICICI	0.890	0.170	P-value > 0.05	H_0 is accepted	**test: K-W test**
	LICI	0.879	0.127	P-value > 0.05	H_0 is accepted	
	MAX	0.907	0.262	P-value > 0.05	H_0 is accepted	
	SBI	*0.778*	*0.008*	*P-value < 0.05*	*H_0 is rejected*	

Source Compilation of data collected from IRDA Annual Reports (IRDAI, 2012, 2015) using SPSS 20.0

(b) Population variances should be homogenous

The assumption is tested based on following hypothesis

Hypothesis:

- H_0: Population variances are homogenous;
- H_1: Population variances are not homogenous.

In order to test the aforesaid hypothesis, Levene's test is conducted using the following test statistic (W):

$$W = \frac{(N-k)}{(k-1)} \frac{\sum_{i=1}^{k} N_i (Z_{i.} - Z_{..})^2}{\sum_{i=1}^{k} \sum_{i=1}^{N_i} N_i (Z_{ij} - Z_{i.})^2}$$

where

k = number of different groups to which the sample cases belong.
N_i = number of cases in the ith group.
N = total number of cases in all groups.
Y_{ij} = the value of measured variable for the jth case from the ith group.
$$z_{ij} = \begin{cases} \left| (Y_{ij} - \overline{Y}_{i.}) \right| \\ \left| (Y_{ij} - \tilde{Y}_{i.}) \right| \end{cases}$$ Absolute difference of the jth case from the ith group from mean of the ith group and median of the ith group.
$Z_{i.} = \frac{1}{N_i} \sum_{j=1}^{N_i} Z_{ij}$
$Z_{..} = \frac{1}{N} \sum_{i=1}^{k} \sum_{j=1}^{N_i} Z_{ij}$

In the current study, $N = 70$ and $k = 7$. Hence, df1 is 6 ($k - 1$) and df2 is 63 ($N - k$). At (6, 63) DF and 5% level of significance, if probability (P-value) of the test statistic in the F distribution table is less than 0.05, H_0 cannot be accepted and vice versa. Results of Levene's test for the DVs are shown in Table 4.2.

The assumption of Homoscedasticity is not fulfilled for any one of the DVs. The assumption of normality is fulfilled for PC, IGOAS and AI. However, the assumption of homoscedasticity is not fulfilled for

Table 4.2   Results of Levene's test

DV	Levene statistic	P-value	Decision rule	Decision based on H_0	Remarks	Proposed test
PC	22.146	0.000	P-value < 0.05	H_0 is rejected	Population variances are	Welch
TI	29.067	0.000	P-value < 0.05	H_0 is rejected	heteroscedastic. Hence, the	K-W
IGOAS	20.959	0.000	P-value < 0.05	H_0 is rejected	assumption is **not** fulfilled	Welch
II	13.283	0.000	P-value < 0.05	H_0 is rejected		K-W
AI	50.705	0.000	P-value < 0.05	H_0 is rejected		Welch
OAI	41.200	0.000	P-value < 0.05	H_0 is rejected		K-W

Source Compilation of data collected from IRDA Annual Reports (IRDAI, 2012, 2015) using SPSS 20.0

them. Hence, Welch test is most appropriate here to analyse significant difference among the companies.

4.4.1.2   Welch Test

PC, IGOAS and AI are normally distributed across sample companies. However, they are heteroscedastic. Hence, in order to analyse significant difference among the sample companies in terms of these three variables, Welch's test is conducted based on following hypothesis:

Hypothesis

- H_0: There is no significant difference among sample companies in terms of a select variable;
- H_1: There is significant difference among sample companies in terms of a select variable.

In order to test the aforesaid hypothesis, the Welch statistic is calculated as follows:

$$T = \frac{\overline{X}_1 - \overline{X}_2}{\sqrt{\frac{s_1^2}{N_1} + \frac{s_2^2}{N_2}}}$$

where $\overline{X}_j$, S_j and N_j are jth sample mean, sample standard deviation (SD) and sample size.

The DF (v) is associated with Welch-Satterthwaite equation as follows:

$$v \approx \frac{\left(\frac{s_1^2}{N_1} + \frac{s_2^2}{N_2}\right)^2}{\frac{s_1^4}{N_1^2 v_1} + \frac{s_2^4}{N_2^2 v_2}}$$

where
$$v_1 = n_1 - 1$$
$$v_2 = n_2 - 1$$

At df1 ($k - 1$, where k is number of IVs) and df2 (v), and 5% level of significance, if the P-value of 't' in t-distribution table is less than 0.05, H_0 cannot be accepted and vice versa. The result of Welch test is shown in Table 4.3.

The LICI and select PLICs are significantly different in terms of their premium collection, investment in Government and other approved securities and approved investment.

Table 4.3 Results of Welch test

Company	Statistic	df1	df2	P-value	Decision rule	Decision based on H_0	Remarks
PC	17.423	6	27.379	0.000	P-value < 0.05	H_0 is rejected	Significant difference exists among the select companies in terms of PC, IGOAS and AI
IGOAS	11.695	6	25.722	0.000	P-value < 0.05	H_0 is rejected	
AI	6.917	6	26.909	0.000	P-value < 0.05	H_0 is rejected	

Source Compilation of data collected from IRDA Annual Reports (IRDAI, 2012, 2015) using SPSS 20.0

4.4.1.3   Kruskal–Wallis Test

TI, II and OAI are not normally distributed across the sample companies. Hence, parametric one-way ANOVA cannot be applied to test significant difference among the companies for these three variables. However, as a remedial measure, K-W test can be applied here based on the following hypothesis:

Hypothesis

- H_0: There is no significant difference among sample companies in terms of a select variable;
- H_1: There is significant difference among sample companies in terms of a select variable.

In order the test the above hypothesis, the test statistic (H) is formulated as follows:

$$H = (N - 1) \frac{\sum_{i=1}^{g} n_i (\bar{r}_{i.} - \bar{r})^2}{\sum_{i=1}^{g} \sum_{j=1}^{n_i} (r_{ij} - \bar{r})^2}$$

where

n_i is the number of observations in each group;
r_{ij} is the rank of observation j in ith group;
N is the total number of observations across all groups;
$\bar{r}_i$ is the average rank of all observation in group I;
$\bar{r}$ is the average of all r_{ij}.

H can be approximated using chi-square distribution with $(g - 1)$ df where g is number of groups. Here, at 6 df and 5% level of significance, if the P-value of H in chi-square distribution table is less than 0.05, H_0 cannot be accepted and vice versa. Results of K-W test for the three above-mentioned variables are shown in Table 4.4.

The LICI and the other six PLICs are significantly different in terms of total investment, infrastructure investment and other than approved investment.

It may be concluded that all the select life insurers are significantly different among themselves in terms of select parameters. In the following

Table 4.4   Results of K-W test

Company	TI	II	OTAI
Chi-square	33.313	29.160	42.152
P-value	0.000	0.000	0.000
Decision rule	P-value < 0.05	P-value < 0.05	P-value < 0.05
Decision based on H_0	H_0 is rejected	H_0 is rejected	H_0 is rejected
Remarks	Significant difference exists among the select companies in terms of TI, II and OAI		

Source Compilation of data collected from IRDA Annual Reports (IRDAI, 2012, 2015) using SPSS 20.0

section, an attempt has been made to group individual life insurers into homogenous subsets based on pair-wise difference between them.

4.4.2   Grouping Select Life Insurance Companies

In the previous section, it has been observed that select life insurers are significantly different among themselves in terms of PC, TI, IGOAS, II, AI and OAI. In order to group the life insurers into homogenous subsets, two post hoc tests to Welch test and K-W test are conducted. Appropriate post hoc test to Welch is Games-Howell test applied to PC, IGOAS and AI, while appropriate post hoc test to K-W test is Dunn test applicable for TI, II and OAI. Results of these tests are discussed below.

4.4.2.1   Games-Howell Test

Pair-wise significant difference among select life insurers is tested based on the following hypothesis:

Hypothesis

- H_0: A pair of two companies is not significantly different in terms of a select variable;
- H_1: A pair of two companies is significantly different in terms of a select variable.

The variables under consideration are PC, IGOAS and AI. In order to test the above hypothesis, the Games-Howell test statistic is calculated as (absolute mean difference between two companies/standard error). At

5% significance level if the P-value of test statistic in t-distribution table is less than 0.05, H_0 cannot be accepted and vice versa. The results of the test for three select variables are discussed as below.

(a) Pair-wise difference in terms of premium collection

The pairs of companies, which are significantly different in terms of their premium collection, are projected in Table 4.5.

It is observed that the LICI is significantly different from other PLICs. At the same time, ICICI is significantly different from BIRLA and MAX. Based on the results of the table, the companies can be grouped into four homogenous subsets as shown in Table 4.6.

LICI being an outlier in the market earns very high premium. However, they are significantly different from the ICICI, which earns high premium. On the other end, BIRLA and MAX are mobilising a low premium. Rest of the companies are collecting a moderate premium.

Table 4.5 Companies with Significant Pair-wise Difference (PC)

Company_1	Company_2	Absolute mean difference $(I - J)$	Std. error	P-value
LICI	ICICI	152,115.29400	16,978.30761	0.000
LICI	BAJAJ	156,792.14000	16,931.65760	0.000
LICI	SBI	156,420.51700	16,963.98655	0.000
LICI	HDFC	157,387.30700	16,947.18281	0.000
LICI	BIRLA	160,009.27100	16,909.15501	0.000
LICI	MAX	159,875.13600	16,917.37798	0.000
ICICI	BIRLA	152,115.29400	16,978.30761	0.000
ICICI	MAX	7759.84200	1834.74498	0.013

Source Compilation of data collected from IRDA Annual Reports (IRDAI, 2012, 2015) using SPSS 20.0

Table 4.6 Homogenous subsets among life insurers (PC)

Subset_1 (very high premium)	Subset_2 (high premium)	Subset_3 (moderate premium)	Subset_4 (low premium)
LICI	ICICI	BAJAJ SBI HDFC	BIRLA MAX

Source Table 4.5

(b) Pair-wise difference in terms of investment in Government and other approved securities

The pairs of companies, which are significantly different in terms of their investment in Government and other approved securities, are shown in Table 4.7.

Only the LICI is significantly different from other six PLICs, which leads to formation of only two subsets (Table 4.8).

The quantum of investment in Government and other approved securities by the LICI is much higher than that of other six PLICs.

(c) Pair-wise difference in terms of approved investment

The pairs of companies, which are significantly different in terms of their approved investments, are projected in Table 4.9.

Table 4.7 Companies with significant pair-wise difference (IGOAS)

Company_1	Company_2	Absolute mean difference $(I - J)$	Std. error	P-value
LICI	ICICI	495,222.44900	69,384.28661	0.001
LICI	BAJAJ	495,693.36400	69,384.96759	0.001
LICI	SBI	493,026.63300	69,397.26243	0.001
LICI	HDFC	495,995.11400	69,382.45428	0.001
LICI	BIRLA	498,022.48900	69,378.33288	0.001
LICI	MAX	496,043.37400	69,383.41491	0.001

Source Compilation of data collected from IRDA Annual Reports (IRDAI, 2012, 2015) using SPSS 20.0

Table 4.8 Homogenous subsets among life insurers (IGOAS)

Subset_1 (very high investment in government and other approved securities)	Subset_2 (moderate investment in government and other approved securities)
LICI	ICICI
	BAJAJ
	SBI
	HDFC
	BIRLA
	MAX

Source Table 4.7

Table 4.9 Companies with Significant Pair-wise Difference (AI)

Company_1	Company_2	Absolute mean difference $(I - J)$	Std. error	P-value
LICI	ICICI	266,087.76200	64,828.19919	0.028
LICI	BAJAJ	284,575.41000	64,476.55170	0.019
LICI	SBI	283,981.82000	64,555.36522	0.019
LICI	HDFC	286,717.06200	64,491.99049	0.018
LICI	BIRLA	291,320.96100	64,397.85276	0.016
LICI	MAX	296,384.10700	64,373.28964	0.015
ICICI	MAX	30,296.34500	7992.86011	0.040

Source Compilation of data collected from IRDA Annual Reports (IRDAI, 2012, 2015) using SPSS 20.0

While the LICI is significantly different from other six PLICs, the ICICI is also significantly different from MAX, which gives rise to four subsets (Table 4.10).

In the above table, LICI with a very high approved investment is at one end, while MAX with a very low approved investment is on the other. ICICI is inclined to the LICI in terms of their approved investments, while rest of the companies stay in the middle.

Table 4.10 Homogenous subsets among life insurers (AI)

Subset_1 (very high approved investment)	Subset_2 (high approved investment)	Subset_3 (moderate approved investment)	Subset_4 (low approved investment)
LICI	ICICI	BAJAJ SBI HDFC BIRLA	MAX

Source Table 4.9

4.4.2.2   Dunn Test

Pair-wise significant difference among select life insurers is tested based on the following hypothesis:

Hypothesis

- H_0: Probability distribution of one insurer is not significantly different from that of the other;
- H_1: Probability distribution of one insurer is significantly different from that of the other.

Dunn test performs $k \, (k-1)$ tests for each pair of companies. Here $k = 7$. Hence, totally 42 tests are to be performed using Z-statistic. If at 5% level of significance, the probability of the Z-statistic in normal distribution table is less than 0.05, H_0 cannot be accepted and vice versa. Dunn test is applicable for TI, II and OAI. The results of the test for the three select variables are discussed below.

(a) Pair-wise difference in terms of total investment

As discussed earlier, there are a total 42 pairs between which the tests are performed. However, the pairs where two companies are significantly different from one another are shown in Table 4.11.

The LICI is significantly different from five out of six PLICs. It is not significantly different from the ICICI. Two subsets can be formed from such relationship (Table 4.12).

Table 4.11 Companies with significant pair-wise difference (TI)

Company_1	Company_2	Test statistic	P-value
LICI	BAJAJ	33.2	0.006
LICI	SBI	32.1	0.009
LICI	HDFC	35.6	0.002
LICI	BIRLA	41.1	0.000
LICI	MAX	45.8	0.000

Source Compilation of data collected from IRDA Annual Reports (IRDAI, 2012, 2015) using SPSS 20.0

Table 4.12
Homogenous subsets
among life insurers (TI)

Subset_1 (very high total investment)	Subset_2 (moderate total investment)
LICI	BAJAJ
ICICI	SBI
	HDFC
	BIRLA
	MAX

Source Table 4.11

Two subsets are created. In the first subset, there are LICI and ICICI with very high total investment. However, the rests are in the other subset with moderate investments.

(b) Pair-wise difference in terms of infrastructure investment

Life insurers with significant pair-wise difference are projected in Table 4.13.

LICI is significantly different from all the PLICs, which lead to only two subsets (Table 4.14).

LICI being only public sector company in the industry makes a huge infrastructure investment. However, infrastructure investments of the PLICs are more or less same.

(c) Pair-wise difference in terms of other than approved investments

The pairs where two companies are having significant difference are shown in Table 4.15.

Table 4.13 Companies with significant pair-wise difference (II)

Company_1	Company_2	Test statistic	P-value
LICI	ICICI	31.7	0.010
LICI	BAJAJ	33.3	0.005
LICI	SBI	32.5	0.007
LICI	HDFC	32.8	0.007
LICI	BIRLA	46.4	0.000
LICI	MAX	33.3	0.005

Source Compilation of data collected from IRDA Annual Reports (IRDAI, 2012, 2015) using SPSS 20.0

Table 4.14
Homogenous subsets
among life insurers (II)

Subset_1 (very high infrastructure investment)	Subset_2 (moderate infrastructure investment)
LICI	ICICI
	BAJAJ
	SBI
	HDFC
	BIRLA
	MAX

Source Table 4.13

Table 4.15 Companies with significant pair-wise difference (OAI)

Company_1	Company_2	Test statistic	P-value
LICI	SBI	36.8	0.001
LICI	HDFC	42.8	0.000
LICI	BIRLA	37.3	0.001
LICI	MAX	50.0	0.000
ICICI	MAX	32.9	0.006

Source Compilation of data collected from IRDA Annual Reports (IRDAI, 2012, 2015) using SPSS 20.0

LICI is significantly different from SBI, HDFC, BIRLA and MAX, while ICICI is significantly different from only MAX. It gives rise to three homogenous subsets (Table 4.16).

It is observed that LICI, ICICI and BAJAJ make a high other than approved investment, while this investment is really low for MAX. Other companies fall in between.

Table 4.16 Homogenous subsets among life insurers (OAI)

Subset_1 (high other than approved investment)	Subset_3 (moderate other than approved investment)	Subset_4 (low other than approved investment)
LICI	SBI	MAX
ICICI	HDFC	
BAJAJ	BIRLA	

Source Table 4.15

4.4.3   Studying Impact of Recession on the Performance of Life Insurance Companies

Indian economy witnessed global economic recession during 2008–2009. The entire financial sector including life insurance sector was adversely affected. Impact of global economic recession on premium collection, total investment and four sectorial investment is analysed by segmenting the entire study period into two segments—pre-recession period (2003–2004 to 2008–2009) and post-recession period (2009–2010 to 2013–2014). Significant difference between these two periods with respect to the select parameters would indicate impact of recession on those parameters.

4.4.3.1   Impact of Recession on Premium Collection

In order to analyse the impact of recession on premium collection, independent sample t-test is made to find out significant difference in premium collection in these two periods subject to fulfilment of certain assumptions.

(a) Assumptions

There are mainly two important assumptions that must be fulfilled for conducting independent sample t-test. (i) DV (in this case premium) should be approximately normally distributed across IVs (here periods) (also known as assumption of normality); (b) population variances must be homogenous (assumption of Homoscedasticity). Assumption of normality is tested using S-W test.

Hypothesis

- H_0: Premium collection is normally distributed across pre- and post-recession period;
- H_1: Premium collection is not normally distributed across pre- and post-recession period.

Results of the test are as follows (Table 4.17).

Table 4.17   Results of Shapiro Wilk's test (impact of recession on PC)

Company	Period	Statistic	P-value	Decision rule	Decision based on H_0	Remarks
LICI	Pre-recession	0.911	0.471	P-value > 0.05	H_0 is accepted	Distribution of premium collection is normally distributed across periods for all companies
	Post-recession	0.910	0.465	P-value > 0.05	H_0 is accepted	
ICICI	Pre-recession	0.922	0.542	P-value > 0.05	H_0 is accepted	
	Post-recession	0.932	0.607	P-value > 0.05	H_0 is accepted	
BAJAJ	Pre-recession	0.926	0.569	P-value > 0.05	H_0 is accepted	
	Post-recession	0.946	0.710	P-value > 0.05	H_0 is accepted	
SBI	Pre-recession	0.917	0.509	P-value > 0.05	H_0 is accepted	
	Post-recession	0.815	0.106	P-value > 0.05	H_0 is accepted	
HDFC	Pre-recession	0.937	0.642	P-value > 0.05	H_0 is accepted	
	Post-recession	0.963	0.825	P-value > 0.05	H_0 is accepted	
BIRLA	Pre-recession	0.908	0.457	P-value > 0.05	H_0 is accepted	
	Post-recession	0.972	0.889	P-value > 0.05	H_0 is accepted	
MAX	Pre-recession	0.937	0.648	P-value > 0.05	H_0 is accepted	
	Post-recession	0.978	0.925	P-value > 0.05	H_0 is accepted	

Source Compilation of data collected from IRDA Annual Reports (IRDAI, 2012, 2015) using SPSS 20.0

Assumption of normality is fulfilled. Assumption of Homoscedasticity is tested using Levene's test based on following hypothesis (Table 4.18):

Hypothesis

- H_0: Population variances for premium collection are homogenous;
- H_1: Population variances for premium collection are not homogenous.

Table 4.18 Results of Levene's test (impact of recession on PC)

Company	F	P-value	Decision rule	Decision based on H_0	Remarks
LICI	4.418	0.069	P-value > 0.05	H_0 is accepted	Population
ICICI	6.086	0.039	P-value < 0.05	H_0 is rejected	variances of all
BAJAJ	3.043	0.119	P-value > 0.05	H_0 is accepted	the companies are
SBI	3.975	0.081	P-value > 0.05	H_0 is accepted	homogenous,
HDFC	0.062	0.810	P-value > 0.05	H_0 is accepted	except for ICICI
BIRLA	10.125	0.013	P-value < 0.05	H_0 is rejected	and BIRLA
MAX	1.668	0.233	P-value > 0.05	H_0 is accepted	

Source Compilation of data collected from IRDA Annual Reports (IRDAI, 2012, 2015) using SPSS 20.0

Assumption of Homoscedasticity is fulfilled for all companies, except ICICI and BIRLA. While t-test is to be conducted for all the companies, for these two companies equal variances are not assumed.

(b) t-test

Significant difference in premium collection in pre- and post-recession period is analysed based on following hypothesis:

Hypothesis

- H_0: Significant difference in premium collection does not exist in pre- and post-recession era;
- H_1: Significant difference in premium collection exists in pre- and post-recession era.

If equal variances are assumed, the hypothesis is tested using t-test with the help of following test statistics (t)

$$t = \frac{\overline{x}_1 - \overline{x}_2}{s_p\sqrt{\frac{1}{n_1} + \frac{1}{n_2}}}$$

where

$$s_p = \sqrt{\frac{(n_1-1)s_1^2 + (n_2-1)s_2^2}{n_1+n_2-2}}$$

Table 4.19   Results of t-test (impact of recession on PC)

Company	t	df	P-value	Decision rule	Decision based on H_0	Remarks
Equal variances assumed						Significant
LICI	−4.826	8	0.001	P-value < 0.05	H_0 is rejected	difference in
BAJAJ	−1.083	8	0.310	P-value > 0.05	H_0 is accepted	premium
SBI	−5.557	8	0.001	P-value < 0.05	H_0 is rejected	collection
HDFC	−5.274	8	0.001	P-value < 0.05	H_0 is rejected	exists in pre-
MAX	−5.744	8	0.000	P-value < 0.05	H_0 is rejected	and
Equal variances not assumed						post-recession
ICICI	−2.270	5.232	0.070	P-value > 0.05	H_0 is accepted	era for all the companies,
BIRLA	−4.325	4.575	0.009	P-value < 0.05	H_0 is rejected	barring ICICI and BAJAJ

Source Compilation of data collected from IRDA Annual Reports (IRDAI, 2012, 2015) using SPSS 20.0

$\overline{x}_1$ = mean of first sample;
$\overline{x}_2$ = mean of second sample;
n_1 = sample size of first sample;
n_2 = sample size of second sample;
s_1 = standard deviation (SD) of first sample;
s_2 = SD of second sample;
s_p = pooled SD.

At 8 df $[n_1 (5) + n_2 (5) − 2]$ and 5% level of significance, if the P-value of t in the t-distribution table is less than 0.05, H_0 cannot be accepted and vice versa. If equal variances are not assumed, test statistics and df are same as that of Welch test (discussed in Sect. 4.4.1.2). Results of t-test for all the companies under consideration are shown in Table 4.19.

Recession had significantly impacted premium collection of all the companies under consideration, except ICICI and BAJAJ. Premium collection of these two companies did not change significantly due to recession.

4.4.3.2   Impact of Recession on Total Investment
Impact of recession on total investment of select companies is tested using independent sample t-test subject to fulfilment of the assumption of normality and Homoscedasticity.

(a) Assumptions

Hypothesis

- H_0: Total investment is normally distributed across pre- and post-recession period;
- H_1: Total investment is not normally distributed across pre- and post-recession period.

Assumption of normality is tested using S-W test as shown in Table 4.20.

Assumption of normality is fulfilled for all the companies except BAJAJ. Hence, impact of recession on TI for BAJAJ is tested using Mann-Whitney (M-W) test. However, for all other companies, t-test is to be conducted. On the other hand, assumption of Homoscedasticity is tested using Levene's test based on following hypothesis (Table 4.21):

Hypothesis

- H_0: Population variances for total investment are homogenous;
- H_1: Population variances for total investment are not homogenous.

Assumption of Homoscedasticity is fulfilled for all the companies. Hence, for all the companies (except BAJAJ), equal variances are to be assumed while conducting t-test.

(b) t-test

Hypothesis

- H_0: Significant difference in total investment does not exist in pre- and post-recession era;
- H_1: Significant difference in total investment exists in pre- and post-recession era.

Results of t-test (assuming equal variances) for all the companies, except BAJAJ, are shown in Table 4.22.

It is observed that recession had significantly impacted total investment of LICI, ICICI, SBI, HDFC, BIRLA and MAX.

Table 4.20   Results of Shapiro Wilk's test (impact of recession on TI)

Company	Period	Statistic	P-value	Decision rule	Decision based on H_0	Remarks
LICI	Pre-recession	0.973	0.893	P-value > 0.05	H_0 is accepted	Distribution of total investment is normally distributed across periods, for all the companies except for BAJAJ
	Post-recession	0.991	0.984	P-value > 0.05	H_0 is accepted	
ICICI	Pre-recession	0.935	0.631	P-value > 0.05	H_0 is accepted	
	Post-recession	0.968	0.862	P-value > 0.05	H_0 is accepted	
BAJAJ	Pre-recession	0.944	0.694	P-value > 0.05	H_0 is accepted	
	Post-recession	**0.752**	**0.031**	**P-value < 0.05**	**H_0 is rejected**	
SBI	Pre-recession	0.909	0.460	P-value > 0.05	H_0 is accepted	
	Post-recession	0.981	0.940	P-value > 0.05	H_0 is accepted	
HDFC	Pre-recession	0.935	0.627	P-value > 0.05	H_0 is accepted	
	Post-recession	0.980	0.934	P-value > 0.05	H_0 is accepted	
BIRLA	Pre-recession	0.938	0.652	P-value > 0.05	H_0 is accepted	
	Post-recession	0.976	0.914	P-value > 0.05	H_0 is accepted	
MAX	Pre-recession	0.919	0.523	P-value > 0.05	H_0 is accepted	
	Post-recession	0.993	0.990	P-value > 0.05	H_0 is accepted	

Source Compilation of data collected from IRDA Annual Reports (IRDAI, 2012, 2015) using SPSS 20.0

(c) Mann-Whitney test

Assumption of normality is not fulfilled for BAJAJ. Hence, any parametric tests (such as t-test) cannot be conducted to test significant difference of total investment of BAJAJ in pre- and post-recession era. Hence,

Table 4.21 Results of Levene's test (impact of recession on TI)

Company	F	P-value	Decision rule	Decision based on H_0	Remarks
LICI	1.035	0.339	P-value > 0.05	H_0 is accepted	Population
ICICI	1.844	0.212	P-value > 0.05	H_0 is accepted	variances of all the
SBI	1.790	0.218	P-value > 0.05	H_0 is accepted	companies are
HDFC	4.433	0.068	P-value > 0.05	H_0 is accepted	homogenous
BIRLA	0.010	0.923	P-value > 0.05	H_0 is accepted	
MAX	3.161	0.113	P-value > 0.05	H_0 is accepted	

Source Compilation of data collected from IRDA Annual Reports (IRDAI, 2012, 2015) using SPSS 20.0

Table 4.22 Results of t-test (impact of recession on TI)

Company	t	df	P-value	Decision rule	Decision based on H_0	Remarks
Equal variances assumed						Significant
LICI	−5.344	8	0.001	P-value < 0.05	H_0 is rejected	difference in
ICICI	−7.896	8	0.000	P-value < 0.05	H_0 is rejected	total investment
SBI	−6.799	8	0.000	P-value < 0.05	H_0 is rejected	exists in pre-
HDFC	−5.136	8	0.001	P-value < 0.05	H_0 is rejected	and
BIRLA	−7.834	8	0.000	P-value < 0.05	H_0 is rejected	post-recession
MAX	−5.490	8	0.001	P-value < 0.05	H_0 is rejected	era for all the
						companies

Source Compilation of data collected from IRDA Annual Reports (IRDAI, 2012, 2015) using SPSS 20.0

non-parametric M-W test is to be conducted based on the following hypothesis:

Hypothesis

- H_0: Significant difference in total investment does not exist in pre- and post-recession era;
- H_1: Significant difference in total investment exists in pre- and post-recession era.

The above hypothesis is tested based on following test statistics (U):

$$U = \text{Smaller value of } U_1 = n_1 n_2 + [n_1(n_1 + 1)]/2 - R_1 \text{ or,}$$

$$U_2 = n_1 n_2 + [n_1(n_1 + 1)]/2 - R_2$$

where

n_1 = sample size in Group-1;
n_2 = sample size of Group-2;
R_1 = sum of ranks in Group-1;
R_2 = sum of ranks in Group-2.

Standardised test statistic $Z = (U - m_u)/\sigma_u$.
where

$m_u = n_1 n_2/2$ and
$\sigma_u = \sqrt{[n_1 n_2(n_1 + n_2 + 1)/12]}$

At 5% level of significance, if the P-value of Z in the normal distribution table is less than 0.05, H_0 cannot be accepted and vice versa. Result of M-W test is shown in Table 4.23.

It is observed that recession had significantly impacted total investment of BAJAJ.

4.4.3.3   *Impact of Recession on Investment in Government and Other Approved Securities*

Impact of recession on IGOAS is analysed subject to fulfilment of the assumptions of normality and Homoscedasticity.

Table 4.23   Results of M-W test (impact of recession on TI)

Company	BAJAJ
Mann-Whitney U	0.000
Wilcoxon W	15.000
Z	−2.611
P-value	0.009
Decision rule	P-value < 0.05
Decision based on H_0	H_0 is rejected
Remarks	Total investment of BAJAJ in pre- and post-recession era is significantly different

Source Compilation of data collected from IRDA Annual Reports (IRDAI, 2012, 2015) using SPSS 20.0

(a) Assumptions

Hypothesis

- H_0: Investment in Government and other approved securities is normally distributed across pre- and post-recession period;
- H_1: Investment in Government and other approved securities is not normally distributed across pre- and post-recession period.

Assumption of normality is tested using S-W test as shown in Table 4.24.

Assumption of normality is fulfilled for all the companies under consideration. However, assumption of Homoscedasticity is tested using Levene's test based on the following hypothesis (Table 4.25):

Hypothesis

- H_0: Population variances for investment in Government and other approved securities are homogenous;
- H_1: Population variances for investment in Government and other approved securities are not homogenous.

Assumption of Homoscedasticity is fulfilled only for LICI. However, for all other companies, the assumption is not met.

(b) t-test

Since assumption of Homoscedasticity is met only for LICI, equal variances are assumed only for this company. However, for other companies, t-test is to be conducted without the assumption of equal variances.

Hypothesis

- H_0: Significant difference in IGOAS does not exist in pre- and post-recession era;
- H_1: Significant difference in IGOAS exists in pre- and post-recession era.

Results of t-test for all the companies under consideration are shown in Table 4.26.

Table 4.24 Results of Shapiro Wilk's test (impact of recession on IGOAS)

Company	Period	Statistic	P-value	Decision rule	Decision based on H_0	Remarks
LICI	Pre-recession	0.987	0.967	P-value > 0.05	H_0 is accepted	Distribution of IGOAS is normally distributed across periods for all the companies
	Post-recession	0.955	0.773	P-value > 0.05	H_0 is accepted	
ICICI	Pre-recession	0.946	0.710	P-value > 0.05	H_0 is accepted	
	Post-recession	0.960	0.806	P-value > 0.05	H_0 is accepted	
BAJAJ	Pre-recession	0.906	0.445	P-value > 0.05	H_0 is accepted	
	Post-recession	0.933	0.616	P-value > 0.05	H_0 is accepted	
SBI	Pre-recession	0.876	0.292	P-value > 0.05	H_0 is accepted	
	Post-recession	0.957	0.785	P-value > 0.05	H_0 is accepted	
HDFC	Pre-recession	0.951	0.746	P-value > 0.05	H_0 is accepted	
	Post-recession	0.948	0.723	P-value > 0.05	H_0 is accepted	
BIRLA	Pre-recession	0.889	0.351	P-value > 0.05	H_0 is accepted	
	Post-recession	0.962	0.823	P-value > 0.05	H_0 is accepted	
MAX	Pre-recession	0.948	0.723	P-value > 0.05	H_0 is accepted	
	Post-recession	0.944	0.695	P-value > 0.05	H_0 is accepted	

Source Compilation of data collected from IRDA Annual Reports (IRDAI, 2012, 2015) using SPSS 20.0

Recession had significantly impacted the investment Government and other approved securities by all the companies under consideration.

4.4.3.4   Impact of Recession on Infrastructure Investment

Impact of recession on infrastructure investment by the select companies is tested using independent sample t-test subject to fulfilment of the assumption of normality and Homoscedasticity.

Table 4.25   Results of Levene's test (impact of recession on IGOAS)

Company	F	P-value	Decision rule	Decision based on H_0	Remarks
LICI	2.947	0.124	P-value > 0.05	H_0 is accepted	Population variances of all the companies are not homogenous. However, population variance of LICI is homogenous
ICICI	8.626	0.019	P-value < 0.05	H_0 is rejected	
BAJAJ	7.781	0.024	P-value < 0.05	H_0 is rejected	
SBI	6.597	0.033	P-value < 0.05	H_0 is rejected	
HDFC	7.443	0.026	P-value < 0.05	H_0 is rejected	
BIRLA	6.380	0.035	P-value < 0.05	H_0 is rejected	
MAX	7.352	0.027	P-value < 0.05	H_0 is rejected	

Source Compilation of data collected from IRDA Annual Reports (IRDAI, 2012, 2015) using SPSS 20.0

Table 4.26   Results of t-test (impact of recession on IGOAS)

Company	t	df	P-value	Decision rule	Decision based on H_0	Remarks
Equal variances assumed						Significant difference in investment in Government and other approved securities exists in pre- and post-recession era for all the companies
LICI	−4.000	8	0.004	P-value < 0.05	H_0 is rejected	
Equal variances not assumed						
ICICI	−4.012	4.554	0.012	P-value < 0.05	H_0 is rejected	
BAJAJ	−3.530	4.401	0.021	P-value < 0.05	H_0 is rejected	
SBI	−4.145	4.802	0.010	P-value < 0.05	H_0 is rejected	
HDFC	−3.769	4.400	0.016	P-value < 0.05	H_0 is rejected	
BIRLA	−5.251	4.751	0.004	P-value < 0.05	H_0 is rejected	
MAX	−3.353	4.294	0.026	P-value < 0.05	H_0 is rejected	

Source Compilation of data collected from IRDA Annual Reports (IRDAI, 2012, 2015) using SPSS 20.0

(a) Assumptions

Hypothesis

- H_0: Infrastructure investment is normally distributed across pre- and post-recession period;
- H_1: Infrastructure investment is not normally distributed across pre- and post-recession period.

Assumption of normality is tested using S-W test as shown in Table 4.27.

Table 4.27   Results of Shapiro Wilk's test (impact of recession on II)

Company	Period	Statistic	P-value	Decision rule	Decision based on H_0	Remarks
LICI	Pre-recession	0.925	0.564	P-value > 0.05	H_0 is accepted	Distributions of II are normally distributed across periods for all the companies
	Post-recession	0.816	0.109	P-value > 0.05	H_0 is accepted	
ICICI	Pre-recession	0.950	0.741	P-value > 0.05	H_0 is accepted	
	Post-recession	0.934	0.622	P-value > 0.05	H_0 is accepted	
BAJAJ	Pre-recession	0.952	0.753	P-value > 0.05	H_0 is accepted	
	Post-recession	0.913	0.485	P-value > 0.05	H_0 is accepted	
SBI	Pre-recession	0.897	0.393	P-value > 0.05	H_0 is accepted	
	Post-recession	0.853	0.203	P-value > 0.05	H_0 is accepted	
HDFC	Pre-recession	0.987	0.969	P-value > 0.05	H_0 is accepted	
	Post-recession	0.995	0.993	P-value > 0.05	H_0 is accepted	
BIRLA	Pre-recession	0.902	0.422	P-value > 0.05	H_0 is accepted	
	Post-recession	0.864	0.244	P-value > 0.05	H_0 is accepted	
MAX	Pre-recession	0.911	0.473	P-value > 0.05	H_0 is accepted	
	Post-recession	0.958	0.795	P-value > 0.05	H_0 is accepted	

Source Compilation of data collected from IRDA Annual Reports (IRDAI, 2012, 2015) using SPSS 20.0

Assumption of normality is fulfilled for all the companies under consideration. However, the assumption of Homoscedasticity is tested using Levene's test based on the following hypothesis (Table 4.28):

Hypothesis

- H_0: Population variances for infrastructure investment are homogenous;
- H_1: Population variances for infrastructure investment are not homogenous.

It is observed that the assumption of Homoscedasticity is met only for LICI and SBI. However, for other companies, the assumption is not met.

(b) t-test

Since the assumption of Homoscedasticity is met for LICI and SBI, t-test conducted for these two companies assumes equal variances. However, t-test conducted for other companies does not assume equal variances.

Hypothesis

- H_0: Significant difference in II does not exist in pre- and post-recession era;
- H_1: Significant difference in II exists in pre- and post-recession era.

Table 4.28 Results of Levene's test (impact of recession on II)

Company	F	P-value	Decision rule	Decision based on H_0	Remarks
LICI	2.846	0.130	P-value > 0.05	H_0 is accepted	Population variances of all the companies are not homogenous, except for LICI and SBI
ICICI	9.011	0.017	P-value < 0.05	H_0 is rejected	
BAJAJ	5.804	0.043	P-value < 0.05	H_0 is rejected	
SBI	2.814	0.132	P-value > 0.05	H_0 is accepted	
HDFC	5.462	0.048	P-value < 0.05	H_0 is rejected	
BIRLA	7.889	0.023	P-value < 0.05	H_0 is rejected	
MAX	8.687	0.019	P-value < 0.05	H_0 is rejected	

Source Compilation of data collected from IRDA Annual Reports (IRDAI, 2012, 2015) using SPSS 20.0

Table 4.29   Results of t-test (impact of recession on II)

Company	t	df	P-value	Decision rule	Decision based on H_0	Remarks
Equal variances assumed						Significant difference in investment in infrastructure investment exists in pre- and post-recession era for all the companies
LICI	−3.552	8	0.007	P-value < 0.05	H_0 is rejected	
SBI	−2.706	8	0.027	P-value < 0.05	H_0 is rejected	
Equal variances not assumed						
ICICI	−3.599	4.269	0.020	P-value < 0.05	H_0 is rejected	
BAJAJ	−4.322	4.507	0.010	P-value < 0.05	H_0 is rejected	
HDFC	−4.530	4.426	0.008	P-value < 0.05	H_0 is rejected	
BIRLA	−6.479	5.359	0.001	P-value < 0.05	H_0 is rejected	
MAX	−4.211	4.522	0.010	P-value < 0.05	H_0 is rejected	

Source Compilation of data collected from IRDA Annual Reports (IRDAI, 2012, 2015) using SPSS 20.0

Results of t-test for all the select companies are shown in Table 4.29.

Recession had significantly impacted infrastructure investment of the select companies.

4.4.3.5   Impact of Recession on Approved Investment
Impact of recession approved investment of the select companies is analysed with the help of t-test subject to fulfilment of the assumption of normality and Homoscedasticity.

(a) Assumptions

Hypothesis

- H_0: Approved investment is normally distributed across pre- and post-recession period;
- H_1: Approved investment is not normally distributed across pre- and post-recession period.

Assumption of normality is tested using S-W test as shown in Table 4.30.

Table 4.30 Results of Shapiro Wilk's test (impact of recession on AI)

Company	Period	Statistic	P-value	Decision rule	Decision based on H_0	Remarks
LICI	Pre-recession	0.904	0.433	P-value > 0.05	H_0 is accepted	Distributions of AI are normally distributed across periods for all the companies
	Post-recession	0.974	0.898	P-value > 0.05	H_0 is accepted	
ICICI	Pre-recession	0.962	0.822	P-value > 0.05	H_0 is accepted	
	Post-recession	0.875	0.286	P-value > 0.05	H_0 is accepted	
BAJAJ	Pre-recession	0.942	0.680	P-value > 0.05	H_0 is accepted	
	Post-recession	0.949	0.728	P-value > 0.05	H_0 is accepted	
SBI	Pre-recession	0.902	0.420	P-value > 0.05	H_0 is accepted	
	Post-recession	0.908	0.455	P-value > 0.05	H_0 is accepted	
HDFC	Pre-recession	0.935	0.632	P-value > 0.05	H_0 is accepted	
	Post-recession	0.989	0.975	P-value > 0.05	H_0 is accepted	
BIRLA	Pre-recession	0.949	0.730	P-value > 0.05	H_0 is accepted	
	Post-recession	0.952	0.754	P-value > 0.05	H_0 is accepted	
MAX	Pre-recession	0.883	0.323	P-value > 0.05	H_0 is accepted	
	Post-recession	0.952	0.749	P-value > 0.05	H_0 is accepted	

Source Compilation of data collected from IRDA Annual Reports (IRDAI, 2012, 2015) using SPSS 20.0

Assumption of normality is fulfilled for all the companies under consideration. Assumption of Homoscedasticity is analysed using Levene's test based on the following hypothesis (Table 4.31):

Hypothesis

- H_0: Population variances for approved investment are homogenous;
- H_1: Population variances for approved investment are not homogenous.

Table 4.31   Results of Levene's test (impact of recession on AI)

Company	F	P-value	Decision rule	Decision based on H_0	Remarks
LICI	0.143	0.715	P-value > 0.05	H_0 is accepted	Population
ICICI	2.511	0.152	P-value > 0.05	H_0 is accepted	variances of all the
BAJAJ	2.487	0.153	P-value > 0.05	H_0 is accepted	companies are
SBI	1.011	0.344	P-value > 0.05	H_0 is accepted	homogenous
HDFC	3.594	0.095	P-value > 0.05	H_0 is accepted	
BIRLA	0.045	0.837	P-value > 0.05	H_0 is accepted	
MAX	3.898	0.084	P-value > 0.05	H_0 is accepted	

Source Compilation of data collected from IRDA Annual Reports (IRDAI, 2012, 2015) using SPSS 20.0

Assumption of Homoscedasticity is met for all the companies under consideration.

(b) Results of t-test

Hypothesis

- H_0: Significant difference in AI does not exist in pre- and post-recession era;
- H_1: Significant difference in AI exists in pre- and post-recession era.

Results of t-test (under the assumption of equal variances) to test the aforesaid hypothesis for all the companies under consideration are shown in Table 4.32.

Recession had significant impact on the approved investment by all the companies under consideration.

4.4.3.6   *Impact of Recession on Other Than Approved Investment*
Impact of recession on other than approved investment of all the select companies is analysed using independent sample t-test subject to fulfilment of the assumptions of normality and Homoscedasticity.

Table 4.32   Results of t-test (impact of recession on AI)

Company	t	df	P-value	Decision rule	Decision based on H_0	Remarks
Equal variances assumed						Significant
LICI	−7.253	8	0.000	P-value < 0.05	H_0 is rejected	difference in
ICICI	−8.514	8	0.000	P-value < 0.05	H_0 is rejected	approved
BAJAJ	−8.164	8	0.000	P-value < 0.05	H_0 is rejected	investments exists
SBI	−8.223	8	0.000	P-value < 0.05	H_0 is rejected	in pre- and
HDFC	−5.456	8	0.001	P-value < 0.05	H_0 is rejected	post-recession era
BIRLA	−7.959	8	0.000	P-value < 0.05	H_0 is rejected	for all the
MAX	−6.836	8	0.000	P-value < 0.05	H_0 is rejected	companies

Source Compilation of data collected from IRDA Annual Reports (IRDAI, 2012, 2015) using SPSS 20.0

(a) Assumptions

Hypothesis

- H_0: Other than approved investment is normally distributed across pre- and post-recession period;
- H_1: Other than approved investment is not normally distributed across pre- and post-recession period.

Assumption of normality is tested using S-W test as shown in Table 4.33.

Assumption of normality is met for all the companies. Assumption of Homoscedasticity is analysed using Levene's test based on the following hypothesis (Table 4.34):

Hypothesis

- H_0: Population variances for other than approved investment are homogenous;
- H_1: Population variances for other than approved investment are not homogenous.

Table 4.33 Results of Shapiro Wilk's test (impact of recession on OAI)

Company	Period	Statistic	P-value	Decision rule	Decision based on H_0	Remarks
LICI	Pre-recession	0.882	0.321	P-value > 0.05	H_0 is accepted	Distributions of OAI are normally distributed across periods for all the companies
	Post-recession	0.819	0.116	P-value > 0.05	H_0 is accepted	
ICICI	Pre-recession	0.871	0.272	P-value > 0.05	H_0 is accepted	
	Post-recession	0.813	0.103	P-value > 0.05	H_0 is accepted	
BAJAJ	Pre-recession	0.912	0.481	P-value > 0.05	H_0 is accepted	
	Post-recession	0.853	0.204	P-value > 0.05	H_0 is accepted	
SBI	Pre-recession	0.846	0.181	P-value > 0.05	H_0 is accepted	
	Post-recession	0.691	0.008	P-value > 0.05	H_0 is accepted	
HDFC	Pre-recession	0.857	0.219	P-value > 0.05	H_0 is accepted	
	Post-recession	0.941	0.675	P-value > 0.05	H_0 is accepted	
BIRLA	Pre-recession	0.890	0.358	P-value > 0.05	H_0 is accepted	
	Post-recession	0.868	0.258	P-value > 0.05	H_0 is accepted	
MAX	Pre-recession	0.867	0.254	P-value > 0.05	H_0 is accepted	
	Post-recession	0.857	0.217	P-value > 0.05	H_0 is accepted	

Source Compilation of data collected from IRDA Annual Reports (IRDAI, 2012, 2015) using SPSS 20.0

Assumption of Homoscedasticity is met all the companies, except ICICI.

Table 4.34   Results of Levene's test (impact of recession on OAI)

Company	F	P-value	Decision rule	Decision based on H_0	Remarks
LICI	1.275	0.292	P-value > 0.05	H_0 is accepted	Population
ICICI	7.302	0.027	P-value < 0.05	H_0 is rejected	variances of all the
BAJAJ	2.437	0.157	P-value > 0.05	H_0 is accepted	companies are
SBI	1.974	0.198	P-value > 0.05	H_0 is accepted	homogenous,
HDFC	0.004	0.952	P-value > 0.05	H_0 is accepted	except for ICICI
BIRLA	3.372	0.104	P-value > 0.05	H_0 is accepted	
MAX	4.199	0.075	P-value > 0.05	H_0 is accepted	

Source Compilation of data collected from IRDA Annual Reports (IRDAI, 2012, 2015) using SPSS 20.0

(b) Results of t-test

Since assumption of Homoscedasticity is not met for ICICI, t-test is conducted without the assumption of equal variance. However, for other six companies, equal variances are assumed (Table 4.35).

Hypothesis

- H_0: Significant difference in OAI does not exist in pre- and post-recession era;
- H_1: Significant difference in OAI exists in pre- and post-recession era.

It is observed that recession had significant impact on the other than approved investment for BAJAJ, HDFC, BIRLA, MAX and ICICI. However, recession did not pose significant impact on the other than approved investments of LICI and SBI.

4.4.4   Examining the Impact of Ownership Structure on the Performance of Life Insurance Companies

With a view to studying the impact of ownership structure on the performance of life insurers, the companies are segmented into two sectors—(a) public sector companies (only LICI) and (b) private sector companies (23 companies). Out of 23 companies in the private sector, for the current study, only six companies have been selected based on judgemental sampling technique. Hence, average performances of these six

Table 4.35 Results of t-test (impact of recession on OAI)

Company	t	df	P-value	Decision rule	Decision based on H_0	Remarks
Equal variances assumed						Significant difference in other than approved investments exists in pre- and post-recession era for all the companies, barring LICI and SBI
LICI	−0.787	8	0.454	P-value > 0.05	H_0 is accepted	
BAJAJ	−3.039	8	0.016	P-value < 0.05	H_0 is rejected	
SBI	−1.266	8	0.241	P-value > 0.05	H_0 is accepted	
HDFC	−3.158	8	0.013	P-value < 0.05	H_0 is rejected	
BIRLA	−4.852	8	0.001	P-value < 0.05	H_0 is rejected	
MAX	−2.994	8	0.017	P-value < 0.05	H_0 is rejected	
Equal variances not assumed						
ICICI	−2.673	5.502	0.040	P-value < 0.05	H_0 is rejected	

Source Compilation of data collected from IRDA Annual Reports (IRDAI, 2012, 2015) using SPSS 20.0

companies are used to measure the performance of the private sector. Now, significant difference between public sector companies (only LICI) and private sector companies (average of six private sector companies) with respect to select parameters (i.e. PC, TI, IGOAS, II, AI and OAI) would indicate the impact of ownership structure on the performance of life insurance companies. Significant difference between public and sector companies with respect to select parameters is tested using independent sample t-test subject to fulfilment of the assumptions of normality and Homoscedasticity.

4.4.4.1   Assumptions

(a) Dependent variables (in this case the select parameters) are normally distributed across independent groups (public and private)

Hypothesis

- H_0: Data on select parameters (PC, TI, IGOAS, II, AI and OAI) are normally distributed across public and private sector;

- H_1: Data on select parameters (PC, TI, IGOAS, II, AI and OAI) are not normally distributed across public and private sector.

In order to test the above hypotheses for each select parameter, S-W test is shown in Table 4.36.

The assumption of normality is fulfilled for all the select parameters.

(b) Population variances are homogenous

Hypothesis

- H_0: Population variances of select parameters (PC, TI, IGOAS, II, AI and OAI) are homogenous;

Table 4.36 Results of Shapiro Wilk's test (impact of ownership structure on select parameters)

Parameters	Sector	Statistic	P-value	Decision rule	Decision based on H_0	Remarks
PC	Public	0.941	0.569	P-value > 0.05	H_0 is accepted	Data on PC, TI, IGOAS, II, AI and OAI are approximately normally distributed across public and private sector
	Private	0.845	0.051	P-value > 0.05	H_0 is accepted	
TI	Public	0.945	0.604	P-value > 0.05	H_0 is accepted	
	Private	0.904	0.240	P-value > 0.05	H_0 is accepted	
IGOAS	Public	0.928	0.431	P-value > 0.05	H_0 is accepted	
	Private	0.890	0.171	P-value > 0.05	H_0 is accepted	
II	Public	0.924	0.395	P-value > 0.05	H_0 is accepted	
	Private	0.896	0.197	P-value > 0.05	H_0 is accepted	
AI	Public	0.890	0.168	P-value > 0.05	H_0 is accepted	
	Private	0.871	0.104	P-value > 0.05	H_0 is accepted	
OAI	Public	0.879	0.127	P-value > 0.05	H_0 is accepted	
	Private	0.853	0.063	P-value > 0.05	H_0 is accepted	

Source Compilation of data collected from IRDA Annual Reports (IRDAI, 2012, 2015) using SPSS 20.0

Table 4.37   Results of Levene's test (impact of ownership structure on select parameters)

Company	F	P-value	Decision rule	Decision based on H_0	Remarks
PC	22.904	0.000	P-value < 0.05	H_0 is rejected	Population
TI	29.199	0.000	P-value < 0.05	H_0 is rejected	variances of all
IGOAS	20.977	0.000	P-value < 0.05	H_0 is rejected	the companies are
II	13.326	0.002	P-value < 0.05	H_0 is rejected	not homogenous
AI	51.555	0.000	P-value < 0.05	H_0 is rejected	for all the select
OAI	42.309	0.000	P-value < 0.05	H_0 is rejected	parameters

Source Compilation of data collected from IRDA Annual Reports (IRDAI, 2012, 2015) using SPSS 20.0

- H_1: Population variances of select parameters (PC, TI, IGOAS, II, AI and OAI) are not homogenous.

Levene's test is made to test the above hypothesis is shown in Table 4.37.

The assumption of Homoscedasticity is not met for any of the parameters. Hence, while analysing significant difference between public and private sectors with respect to the select parameters, equal variances are not assumed.

4.4.4.2   Results of t-test

It is observed that the assumption of normality is met while the assumption of Homoscedasticity is not met (Sect. 4.4.4.1). Hence, with a view to analysing significant difference between public and private sector life insurers with respect to select parameters (PC, TI, IGOAS, II, AI and OAI), t-test is conducted without assuming homogeneity of population variances based on following hypothesis (Table 4.38):

Hypothesis

- H_0: Public and private sector companies are not significantly different in terms of select parameters;
- H_1: Public and private sector companies are significantly different in terms of select parameters.

Table 4.38 Results of t-test (impact of ownership structure on select parameters)

Company	t	df	P-value	Decision rule	Decision based on H_0	Remarks
Equal variances not assumed						Significant difference exists between public and private sector companies with respect to all the select parameters
PC	9.279	9.071	0.000	P-value < 0.05	H_0 is rejected	
TI	7.030	9.034	0.000	P-value < 0.05	H_0 is rejected	
IGOAS	7.144	9.003	0.000	P-value < 0.05	H_0 is rejected	
II	8.962	9.014	0.000	P-value < 0.05	H_0 is rejected	
AI	4.417	9.074	0.002	P-value < 0.05	H_0 is rejected	
OAI	9.771	9.033	0.000	P-value < 0.05	H_0 is rejected	

Source Compilation of data collected from IRDA Annual Reports (IRDAI, 2012, 2015) using SPSS 20.0

The results suggest that public sector (LICI) and private sector companies (average of six PLICs) are significantly different in terms of PC, TI, IGOAS, II, AI and OAI.

4.4.5 *Analysing the Impact of Select Life Insurance Companies on the Industry*

In the current segment, an attempt has been made to analyse the impact of the LICI and six PLICs on the entire life insurance industry in terms of premium collection, total investment and four sectorial investments. For the purpose of the analysis, industry data with respect to premium collection, total investment and four sectorial investments have been gathered from the IRDA annual reports. Since the data are continuous in nature, the impact of individual companies on the performance of the industry is measured with the help of multiple linear regression analysis (MLRA) considering industry data as dependent variable (DV) and individual company data as independent variables (IVs). MLRA has been conducted keeping in view four specific issues: (a) relationship between company performance and industry performance with respect to select parameters; (b) impact of company performance on industry performance with respect to select parameters; (c) strength of association between company performance and industry performance with respect to select parameters; and (d) significance of the strength of association.

4.4.5.1 *Relationship Between Company Performance and Industry Performance with Respect to Select Parameters*

Relationship between company performance and industry performance is analysed with respect to select parameters, such as premium collection, total investment, investment in Government and other approved securities, infrastructure investment, approved investment and other than approved investment. The relationship under MLRA for each of these parameters can be established as follows:

$$\text{Industry} = \alpha + \beta_1 \text{LICI} + \beta_2 \text{ICICI} + \beta_3 \text{BAJAJ} + \beta_4 \text{SBI} + \beta_5 \text{HDFC}$$
$$+ \beta_6 \text{BIRLA} + B_7 \text{MAX}$$

where α = intercept; $\beta_1,\ldots,\beta_7$ = un-standardised coefficients of individual companies.

$$\hat{\beta} = \frac{\sum (x - \bar{x})(y - \bar{y})}{\sum (y - \bar{y})^2}$$

where

$\hat{\beta}$ is estimated value of un-standardised β;
x = observed value of select IV;
y = observed value of DV;
$\bar{x}$ = mean value of select IV;
$\bar{y}$ = mean value of DV;
Standardised $\beta = \bar{y} - \hat{\beta} \times x$

The standardised β values of select companies for all the aforementioned parameters have been estimated using the above formula and depicted in Table 4.39. The sign and magnitude of the values represent the relationship of an individual company with the industry with respect to a particular parameter.

With respect to premium collection, only BAJAJ negatively influences the industry performance. However, its impact on total premium collection is quite low. On the other hand, the LICI has a high positive relationship with the industry. In terms of total investment, only LICI, ICICI and MAX positively influence industry performance. Among them,

Table 4.39 Relationship between company performance and industry performance with respect to select parameters

Company	Standardised coefficients (β)					
	PC	TI	IGOAS	II	AI	OAI
LICI	0.696	0.208	0.756	0.789	0.002	0.700
ICICI	0.095	1.168	0.164	0.085	0.193	−0.028
BAJAJ	−0.006	−0.422	1.150	0.048	0.006	0.088
SBI	0.062	−0.008	0.143	0.044	−0.228	0.182
HDFC	0.023	−0.306	0.193	0.052	−0.141	−0.015
BIRLA	0.142	−0.347	0.166	0.009	0.734	0.112
MAX	0.014	0.707	−0.421	−0.018	0.435	0.038

Source Compilation of data collected from IRDA Annual Reports (IRDAI, 2012, 2015) using SPSS 20.0

the impact of ICICI seems to be very high. On the other hand, SBI has the least impact on industry performance. In terms of investment in Government and other approved securities, only MAX negatively influences the industry performance. While LICI is still in the market leader in this investment, impact of SBI is negligible. With respect to infrastructure investment as well, only MAX has negative impact on the market. Influence of LICI being highest, BIRLA has least influence on the industry performance. In terms of approved investment, SBI and HDFC negatively influence market performance. BIRLA is projecting maximum influence, while influence of LICI is surprisingly low in this sectorial investment. Finally, in other than approved investment, ICICI and HDFC have negative influence on the market. However, HDFC has least possible impact. Once again, LICI is the market leader in this type of investment.

4.4.5.2   Impact of Company Performance on Industry Performance with Respect to Select Parameters

In order to analyse the impact of company performance on industry performance with respect to select parameters, statistical significance of β in the aforementioned equation are tested with the help of t-test on the basis of following hypothesis:

Hypothesis

- H_0: Significant relationship does not exist between industry performance and performance of a select company with respect to select parameters;

- H_1: Significant relationship exists between industry performance and performance of a select company with respect to select parameters.

In order to test the above hypothesis, the test statistic (t) is calculated as follows:

$$t = \frac{\beta_i}{SE_{\beta i}}$$

where $SE_{\beta i}$ = standard error of the coefficient

At $(n - 2)$ df (where n is number of observations = 10) and 5% level of significance, if the P-value of t in t-distribution table is less than 0.05, H_0 cannot be accepted and vice versa. The results of t-test of all individual coefficients for all the select parameters are shown in Table 4.40.

The results show that in terms of premium collection, investment in Government and other approved securities, infrastructure investment and other than approved investment, only LICI significantly influences industry performances. However, in terms of total investment, only ICICI significantly influences industry performance. In case of approved investment, none of the companies significantly influence the industry performance.

4.4.5.3   Strength of Association Between Company Performance and Industry Performance with Respect to Select Parameters

Strength of association refers to percentage of variance of DV explained by the IVs. If there is only 1 IV, strength of association (r^2) is measured as follows:

$$r^2 = SS_{\text{Reg}}/SS_{\text{Total}}$$

where sum of square $(SS)_{\text{Reg}}$ = total variance explained by the regression equation calculated based on observed and estimated values of DV

SS_{Total} = total variance of the independent variable

Table 4.40 Impact of company performance on industry performance with respect to select parameters

Company	t-statistic	P-value	Decision rule	Decision based on H_0	Remarks
Premium collection					
LICI	10.083	0.010	P-value < 0.05	H_0 is rejected	Significant
ICICI	2.224	0.156	P-value > 0.05	H_0 is accepted	relationship exists
BAJAJ	−0.111	0.921	P-value > 0.05	H_0 is accepted	between LICI
SBI	0.982	0.430	P-value > 0.05	H_0 is accepted	and industry with
HDFC	0.428	0.710	P-value > 0.05	H_0 is accepted	respect to
BIRLA	1.299	0.324	P-value > 0.05	H_0 is accepted	premium
MAX	0.096	0.932	P-value > 0.05	H_0 is accepted	collection
Total investment					
LICI	1.698	0.232	P-value > 0.05	H_0 is accepted	Significant
ICICI	4.400	0.048	P-value < 0.05	H_0 is rejected	relationship exists
BAJAJ	−2.142	0.165	P-value > 0.05	H_0 is accepted	between ICICI
SBI	−0.028	0.980	P-value > 0.05	H_0 is accepted	and industry with
HDFC	−1.891	0.199	P-value > 0.05	H_0 is accepted	respect to total
BIRLA	−0.699	0.557	P-value > 0.05	H_0 is accepted	investment
MAX	2.333	0.145	P-value > 0.05	H_0 is accepted	
Investment in government and other approved securities					
LICI	6.696	0.007	P-value < 0.05	H_0 is rejected	Significant
ICICI	0.927	0.422	P-value > 0.05	H_0 is accepted	relationship exists
BAJAJ	0.799	0.508	P-value > 0.05	H_0 is accepted	between LICI
SBI	0.617	0.581	P-value > 0.05	H_0 is accepted	and industry with
HDFC	0.676	0.548	P-value > 0.05	H_0 is accepted	respect to
BIRLA	1.833	0.164	P-value > 0.05	H_0 is accepted	investment in
MAX	−2.102	0.126	P-value > 0.05	H_0 is accepted	Government and other approved securities
Infrastructure investment					
LICI	67.535	0.000	P-value < 0.05	H_0 is rejected	Significant
ICICI	2.173	0.162	P-value > 0.05	H_0 is accepted	relationship exists
BAJAJ	1.530	0.266	P-value > 0.05	H_0 is accepted	between LICI
SBI	1.891	0.199	P-value > 0.05	H_0 is accepted	and industry with
HDFC	1.880	0.201	P-value > 0.05	H_0 is accepted	respect to
BIRLA	0.332	0.771	P-value > 0.05	H_0 is accepted	infrastructure
MAX	−0.228	0.841	P-value > 0.05	H_0 is accepted	investment
Approved investment					

(continued)

Table 4.40 (continued)

Company	t-statistic	P-value	Decision rule	Decision based on H_0	Remarks
LICI	0.023	0.984	P-value > 0.05	H_0 is accepted	Significant relationship does not exist between any of the select companies and industry with respect to approved investment
ICICI	0.243	0.831	P-value > 0.05	H_0 is accepted	
BAJAJ	0.015	0.989	P-value > 0.05	H_0 is accepted	
SBI	−0.739	0.537	P-value > 0.05	H_0 is accepted	
HDFC	−0.327	0.774	P-value > 0.05	H_0 is accepted	
BIRLA	0.994	0.425	P-value > 0.05	H_0 is accepted	
MAX	1.712	0.229	P-value > 0.05	H_0 is accepted	
Other than approved investment					
LICI	10.200	0.009	P-value < 0.05	H_0 is rejected	Significant relationship exists between LICI and industry with respect to other than approved investment
ICICI	−0.233	0.837	P-value > 0.05	H_0 is accepted	
BAJAJ	1.894	0.199	P-value > 0.05	H_0 is accepted	
SBI	1.466	0.280	P-value > 0.05	H_0 is accepted	
HDFC	−0.213	0.851	P-value > 0.05	H_0 is accepted	
BIRLA	0.853	0.484	P-value > 0.05	H_0 is accepted	
MAX	0.971	0.434	P-value > 0.05	H_0 is accepted	

Source Compilation of data collected from IRDA Annual Reports (IRDAI, 2012, 2015) using SPSS 20.0

In case of MLRA, if IVs are uncorrelated, strength of association (R^2) is measured as:

$$R^2 = \sum_{i=1}^{n} r_i^2$$

where number of IVs $= n$.

However, actually, IVs have correlation among them. In those cases, strength of association is measured in terms of Adjusted R^2 adjusted for the number of IVs and sample size. It lies between 0 and 1. The higher the value of Adjusted R^2, higher is the strength of association between DV and IVs. In our present study, the value of Adjusted R^2 is shown in Table 4.41).

LICI captures around 70% of the market share. In addition to that, six select PLICs are the front runners in terms of their premium collection and total investment. Hence, strength of association of LICI and six PLICs with the industry for all the select parameters is more than 99%.

Table 4.41 Strength of association between company performance and industry performance with respect to select parameters

Parameter	Adjusted R^2
PC	1.000
TI	1.000
IGOAS	0.999
II	1.000
AI	0.997
OAI	0.999

Source Compilation of data collected from IRDA Annual Reports (IRDAI, 2012, 2015) using SPSS 20.0

4.4.5.4 Significance of the Strength of Association

Significance of R^2 is measured with the help of F-test on the basis of following hypothesis:

Hypothesis

- H_0: There is no significant association between industry performance and performance of select companies with respect to select parameters;
- H_1: There is significant association between industry performance and performance of select companies with respect to select parameters.

The test statistic (F) to be estimated to test the above hypothesis is as follows:

$$F = (SS_{Reg}/k)/[(SS_{Total} - SS_{Reg})/(n - k - 1)]$$

where

n = number of observations = 10.
k = number of IVs = 7.

At $(k, n - k - 1)$ df and 5% level of significance, if the P-value of F in the F distribution table is less than 0.05, H0 cannot be accepted and vice versa. The results of F-test for all the select parameters are shown in Table 4.42.

Table 4.42 Significance of the strength of association

Parameter	F-statistic	P-value	Decision rule	Decision based on H_0	Remarks
PC	12,709.111	0.000	P-value < 0.05	H_0 is rejected	There is
TI	5134.775	0.000	P-value < 0.05	H_0 is rejected	significant
IGOAS	1252.644	0.000	P-value < 0.05	H_0 is rejected	association
II	34,437.623	0.000	P-value < 0.05	H_0 is rejected	between
AI	395.022	0.003	P-value < 0.05	H_0 is rejected	industry
OAI	996.111	0.001	P-value < 0.05	H_0 is rejected	performance and performance of select companies with respect to the select parameters

Source Compilation of data collected from IRDA Annual Reports (IRDAI, 2012, 2015) using SPSS 20.0

The above results show that strength of association between performances of the select companies and the performance of the industry is significant for all the select parameters. Hence, the models are fit to explain the relationship between the select companies and industry.

4.4.6   Conclusion

The current chapter empirically analyses the performance of the LICI and six PLICs in terms of select parameters, such as premium collection, total investment, investment in Government and other approved securities, infrastructure investment, approved investment and other than approved investment. It is observed that the companies under consideration are significantly different from one another for these select parameters. LICI being the market leader projected an extra-ordinary performance in terms of almost all the parameters. ICICI is also not far behind LICI. However, BIRLA and MAX lagged behind the other competitors. Global economic recession in 2008–2009 significantly influenced the performances of these seven companies in terms of all the select parameters. However, premium collection of ICICI and BAJAJ did not change significantly in the post-recession era. On the other hand, recession has little impact on the other than approved investments of LICI and SBI. Ownership structure also poses a significant impact on the performance of the companies in terms of all the select parameters. When the performance of the individual companies were compared with the industry performance, it is observed that LICI significantly influences premium collection, investment in Government and other approved securities, infrastructure investment and other than approved investment of the industry, while ICICI has significant influence on the total investment of the industry. However, the next chapter, the final one incorporates a summary of all the chapters, implications, areas of further research and a suitable conclusion on the study.

REFERENCES

IRDAI. (2012). *Handbook on Indian Insurance Statistics, 2011–2012.*
IRDAI. (2015). *Handbook on Indian Insurance Statistics, 2014–2015.*

CHAPTER 5

Concluding Observations and Suggestions

Abstract This chapter, concluding one, presents a summary of findings of previous chapters followed by economic and social implications of the current research. Finally, proposals for further research have been made and suitable conclusion on research findings has been drawn as well. It is finally revealed that during the post-reforms era, performance of the life insurers in terms of premium mobilisation, total investment and other sectorial investments has been quite volatile. On the top of tsshat, global economic recession has made the situation worse for some of the insurance companies. However, a few positive initiatives under-taken by the IRDAI assist the sector to gain back grounds. Despite a falling market share, the LICI still lie ahead of its private peers, probably because of its higher exposure to Government and approved securities. Among the PLICs, ICICI is slowly entering the big league, while SBI, BAJAJ and HDFC are projecting moderate performance. However, the performance of BIRLA and MAX is not satisfactory. They may change their marketing strategies to mobilise more savings from the market. The IRDAI must also be vigilant in monitoring the performance of the insur-ance companies. They should carefully scrutinise the economic scenario in the country and modify the investment portfolio from time to time to ensure security of the savers' fund on the one hand and better return on the other.

© The Author(s), under exclusive license to Springer Nature
Singapore Pte Ltd. 2022
S. P. Patra et al., *Investment Pattern of LICI and Select Private LICs in the Post-reforms Era in India*,
https://doi.org/10.1007/978-981-19-2799-7_5

Keywords IRDAI · LICI · Investment Portfolio · ICICI · SBI · BAJAJ · BIRLA · MAX

5.1   INTRODUCTION

The previous chapter incorporated an empirical discussion on the performances of the LICI and six PLICs with respect to their premium collection, total investment, investment in Government and other approved securities, infrastructure investment, approved investment and other than approved investment. This chapter, the concluding one, at first, makes an attempt to sum up the main issues, which are observed in the previous chapters. Then, it gives a few suggestions stipulating economic and social implications based on the present research work. Finally, some areas for further research have been identified and a suitable conclusion has been drawn from the study.

5.2   SUMMARY OF MAJOR FINDINGS IN PREVIOUS CHAPTERS

A brief summary of **major findings in previous chapters is** pointed out here.

5.2.1   *Chapter 2*

The current chapter conceptually reviews Indian life insurance industry with special emphasis on their investment portfolio.

5.2.1.1   *Evolution*
- The evolution of life insurance business has been discussed in national and global context.
- Evolution of life insurance businesses in India has been discussed by segmenting the whole period into pre-independence era, post-independence era and pre-reforms era.
- Before independence, Indian life insurance industry was dominated by mainly British life insurance companies.
- Back then, it was an urban phenomenon.

- After India's independence, nationalisation of the Life Insurance Corporation of India (LICI) by bringing together numerous small insurance companies was a significant event.
- It led to a surge in premium mobilisation and investible fund.
- In pre-reforms era, the LICI enjoyed complete monopoly in the sector.
- After financial sector reforms, private participation, technology up-gradation, numerous products and after sale service have enhanced the efficiency of the life insurance sector.
- New market-oriented products, such as Unit Linked Product (ULIP), were introduced to tap a potential market looking for increased return on investment.
- Private players were allowed to partner with foreign companies.
- The entire life insurance sector was brought under the ambit of the Insurance Regulatory and Development Authority (IRDAI).
- The IRDAI has increased penetration of life insurance in rural sector.

5.2.1.2 Overview of the Insurance Market
- Currently, 24 companies incorporating 23 private sector companies and one public sector company (LICI) are there in the industry.
- According to Insurance Act 1938, the aggregate holding of a foreign company in an Indian insurance company should not exceed 26%. Currently, out of 23 companies, quite a few companies have collaborated with another foreign company allowing them an aggregate shareholding of less than 26%.

5.2.1.3 Regulatory Framework
- Regulatory framework governing life insurance business has been discussed by dividing them into regulations of pre-independence era, post-independence era and post-reforms era.
- In the pre-independence era, the applicable regulations were made keeping in view the interest British insurance companies operating in India.
- After the enactment of the Indian Insurance Act 1938, insurance companies of Indian origin gained prominence.
- Due to managerial drawbacks, nationalisation of the insurance companies was felt necessary and LICI was formed as per the provisions of LIC Act 1956.

- Insurance sector reforms as per the recommendations of Malhotra Committee and subsequent enactment of the IRDA Act 1999 and establishment of the IRDAI were significant milestone in history of India's life insurance business.

5.2.1.4   Investment Portfolio

- Portfolio of total investible fund of the life insurance businesses has changed over time.
- The chapter elaborates investment portfolio in pre-independence era, post-independence era, pre-reforms era and post-reforms era.
- Total fund of the life insurance companies is divided into three segments, life fund, pension and annuity fund, and ULIP fund.
- While in the pre-reforms era, investments were made in Government and approved securities, in the post-reforms era, it has been extended to infrastructure and social sectors.

5.2.2   Chapter 3

The chapter analyses growth, trend and correlation of premium collection, total investment and sectorial investments (such as investment in Government and other approved securities, infrastructure investments, approved investments and other than approved investments) of LICI and six other private life insurance companies (PLICs) (selected based on judgement sampling technique) during the post-reforms period (2003–04 to 2013–14). The relevant data for the analysis are collected from IRDAI Annual Reports and compiled using statistical software.

5.2.2.1   Analysis of Growth

- Growth of premium collection, total investment and four sectorial investments of the LICI and six PLICs are analysed here.
- LICI has been continuously losing its market share from the private peers in terms of premium collection and total investment.
- Among the private players, the SBI has secured the top position while BIRLA was among the least performers.
- Growth of sectorial investments during the study period was volatile and it reached to its minimum during global economic recession.

- During recession, investment in Government and other approved securities has shown a sudden surge as compared to other sectors, probably due to lack of confidence in other sectors.
- Growth in sectorial investments by the LICI was significantly higher than its private players during recession.
- In terms of average growth in sectorial investments, LICI has outperformed its private peers.
- Among the private players, SBI, BAJAJ and HDFC are the front runners while ICICI lags behind other private insurers considered in the study.

5.2.2.2   *Analysis of Trend*

- Trend of premium collection, total investment and four sectorial investments of the LICI and six PLICs are analysed using log-linear model.
- All the companies under consideration are projecting an increasing trend in terms of all the identified parameters.
- LICI's progress over the years is slow-paced as compared to its private peers.
- Among the private players, ICICI is projecting a promising trend for most of the parameters. However, SBI and BAJAJ are also not far behind ICICI.
- BIRLA is not depicting potential for growth among the private players.
- In terms of CAGR of infrastructure investments or approved investments, rather low-trending companies like BIRLA and MAX reported highest figures.
- In terms of CAGR in other parameters, SBI, BAJAJ and HDFC have secured the highest position.
- LICI has recorded the lowest CAGR under all the parameters.

5.2.2.3   *Correlation Analysis*

- Correlation between premium collection and total investments during the study period for the sample companies is estimated using Pearson's correlation coefficient. Correlations among the companies have also been evaluated with respect to all the select parameters.
- Premium collection and total investments are positively and significantly correlated for all the companies except for BAJAJ.

- Companies have significant positive correlation among themselves in terms of premium collection, total investments and other sectorial investments.
- Premium collection of BAJAJ is not significantly correlated with that of LICI, HDFC and MAX.
- LICI is not significantly correlated with HDFC and BIRLA and SBI is not significantly correlated with BIRLA in terms of other than approved investments.

5.2.3   Chapter 4

In the chapter, divergence among the LICI and select PLICs in terms of their premium collection, total investment and four sectorial investments is analysed and a few homogenous groups have been formed based on their relative nearness. Impact of global economic recession on the select parameters has also been analysed. The chapter also analyses impact of ownership structure on the performance of the company with respect to select parameters. Impact of the select companies on industry performance is finally analysed here.

5.2.3.1   Analysis of Significant Difference

- Significant difference among the LICI and six PLICs in terms of premium collection, total investments and four sectorial investments is analysed using one-way analysis of variance (ANOVA) subject to fulfilment of the assumption of normality (tested using Shapiro-Wilks test) and Homoscedasticity (tested using Levene's test).
- Due to non-fulfilment of assumptions for some of the parameters, one-way ANOVA could not be conducted. As a remedial measure, Welch's test (where the assumption of Homoscedasticity is not fulfilled) and Kruskal–Wallis (K-W) test (where the assumption of normality is not fulfilled) is conducted to find out divergence among the companies.
- It is observed that companies under consideration are significantly different from one another in terms of their premium collection, total investment and four sectorial investments.

5.2.3.2 Grouping of Individual Companies

- Since the assumption of both normality and Homoscedasticity is not fulfilled for any of the parameters, Tukey's Honesty Significant Difference (HSD) test (post hoc test to one-way ANOVA) cannot be conducted to group individual companies into homogenous subsets. Hence, Games-Howell test is conducted for those parameters where Welch test was conducted to find out significant difference and Dunn test is performed for those parameters where K-W test was conducted to find out significance difference.
- LICI being the market leader projected an extra-ordinary performance in terms of almost all the parameters. ICICI is also not far behind LICI.
- BAJAJ, SBI and HDFC reported average performance in terms of total premium mobilisation.
- BIRLA and MAX lagged behind the other competitors.

5.2.3.3 Impact of Recession

- Impact of global economic recession on the performance of select companies with respect to premium collection, total investment and four sectorial investments is measured with the help of t-test by dividing the entire study period into pre-recession and post-recession period subject to fulfilment of applicable assumptions. Where the assumptions are not fulfilled, non-parametric Mann–Whitney (M-W) test has been conducted.
- It is observed that recession significantly influenced the performances of these seven companies in terms of all the select parameters.
- Premium collection of ICICI and BAJAJ did not change significantly in the post-recession era.
- Recession had little impact on the other than approved investments of LICI and SBI.

5.2.3.4 Impact of ownership structure

- Impact of ownership structure on the performance of the select companies in terms of select parameters has been analysed by segmenting the companies into public and private sector.
- Since only one company is there in public sector (LICI), in order to compare its performance with the private sector companies, averages

of six PLICs have been calculated with respect to the select parameters. Performance of LICI with respect to the select parameters is then compared with that of the average performance of the select PLICs.

- Subject to fulfilment of the applicable assumptions, t-test is conducted.
- It is observed that ownership structure also poses a significant impact on the performance of the companies in terms of all the select parameters.

5.2.3.5   *Impact of Industry Performance*
- Impact of the performances of select companies on the performance of the industry with respect to select parameters has been measured using multiple linear regression analysis (MLRA) considering industry performance as dependent variable and performance of select companies as independent variables. When the performance of the individual companies was compared with the industry performance, it is observed that LICI significantly influences premium collection, investment in Government and other approved securities, infrastructure investment, and other than approved investment of the industry, while ICICI has significant influence on the total investment of the industry. The next chapter, the final one incorporates, a summary of all the chapters, implications, areas of further research and a suitable conclusion.

5.3   ECONOMIC AND SOCIAL
IMPLICATIONS: A FEW SUGGESTIONS

On the basis of the research findings, the study offers a few economic and social implications for the regulatory authorities of the life insurance sector and life insurance market participants to optimise premium collection and its appropriate utilisation among different sectors.

- BIRLA and MAX lagged behind its other competitors in terms of premium collection and total investment. They may change their marketing strategy to enhance their total premium collection.

- BIRLA and MAX may also modify their investment strategies to improve their return on investible funds.
- The IRDAI should increase proportion of investment in Government and other approved securities in the investment portfolio in order to ensure security of return from an insurance policy and draw more savers in the market.
- The LICI has always been a safer destination for the small savers. Hence, it has always maintained a good proportion of investment in Government and other approved securities in their investment portfolio. However, in the presence of other private players, the LICI may increase their exposure to other than approved investments in order to survive the competition for return.
- Other than approved investments (investments in equity and equity-related instruments) may increase the total return on a policy if the economic scenario is conducive for such investment. Hence, the IRDAI may strategically increase the proportion of Other than Approved Investment (OAI) in the portfolio to tap a higher return from a growing market.
- Companies should be cautious about the performance of approved investments and suggest the IRDAI about the proportion of this investment in the portfolio.
- Private life insurers are significantly below the LICI in terms of premium collection and total investments even after 20 years of insurance sector reform. They should tap the savings of Indian households by administering advanced technology, innovative product ideas and comprehensive agency network.
- The IRDAI should monitor performance of the securities under four sectorial investments and change the investment portfolio in regular interval in response to the economic scenario and expected performance of these securities.

5.4   AREAS OF FURTHER RESEARCH

A few areas of further research in this field may be made as follows:

- A comparative analysis of the performance of life insurance companies and general insurance companies with respect to premium collection, total investment and investment portfolio;

- Marketing strategy of life insurance business in the rural and urban area in India;
- A comparative analysis of the performances of life insurance companies in India and in select foreign countries;
- Risk management in life insurance business in India;
- Financial performance analysis and efficiency analysis of life insurance companies; and
- Impact of foreign direct investment (FDI) on life insurance industry.

5.5   CONCLUSIONS

After the nationalisation of Indian insurance sector, the LICI enjoyed complete monopoly for nearly 44 years till insurance sector reforms in 2000 and entry of private players in the market. Since then, the LICI has been thriving to gain ground from its private peers. However, in the last 20 years, private entities have become more than successful in understanding pulse of Indian savers and devised their marketing strategies accordingly. As a resultant effect, the market share of the LICI has dropped down from 100% to only 69% in the post-reforms era. Despite its large scale of operation, growth of the LICI had come down to a great extent. There are several parameters that usually indicate the performance of life insurers. Mobilisation of premium and channelisation of investment fund in productive sectors are two important parameters of judging the performance of an insurer. Since investment of mobilised fund is made as per the portfolio prescribed by the IRDA, return earned by an insurer from investing the fund through prescribed channels has also become another parameter of performance evaluation. During the post-reforms era, performance of the life insurers in terms of the aforementioned parameters has been quite volatile. On the top of that, global economic recession in 2008–09 has made the situation worse for some of the insurance companies. However, a few positive initiatives undertaken by the IRDAI, such as scrapping of interest or tariffs and allowing FDI to the extent of 26%, boosted the performance of the sector to some extent. Despite a falling performance of the LICI, still quite a larger percentage of Indian savers trust the company. This might be because of its greater exposure to Government and approved securities or its managerial efficiency sustaining the market for quite some time. That is why, even after falling numbers, the LICI lies much ahead of their private peers in terms of premium mobilisation or return from its investment and significantly controls the industry as a whole. However, private players, such as ICICI Prudential Life Insurance (ICICI), have reported better numbers and entered in the big league because of its managerial efficiencies, innovative product ideas and large group of agency network. Other private life insurers like Bajaj Allianz Life Insurance (BAJAJ), SBI Life (SBI) and HDFC Standard Life (HDFC) have projected moderate performance in the last few years. However, Aditya Birla Sunlife (BIRLA) and Max Life Insurance (MAX) are still struggling to gain a position in India's life insurance market. In order to improve their performance, the companies must change their marketing strategies to mobilise more savings in the form of premium and judiciously invest the same in productive channels. They must tap the latest technological interventions to improve their operations and use the high population to build a comprehensive agency network. The IRDAI must also be vigilant in monitoring the performance of the insurance companies. They should carefully scrutinise the economic scenario in the country and modify the investment portfolio from time to time to ensure security of the savers' fund on the one hand and better return on the other. They must also take positive steps to improve density and penetration of insurance businesses in India.

Bibliography

Books

Adigal, V. S., & Mehta, M. C. (2014). *Changing finance and economic perspectives*. Bharti Publications.

Balachandran, S. (2009). *Life insurance*. Insurance Institute of India.

Bhasin, N. (2007). *Banking and financial market in India 1947 to 2007*. Century Publication.

Bhattacharyya, R. K. (2004). *Money and financial system*. Bhattacharjee Brothers.

Bhole, L. M. (2004). *Financial institutions and market*. TATA McGraw Hill Publishing Company Limited.

Booth, P., Chadburn, R., Haberman, S., James, D., Khorasanee, Z., & Plumb, R. H. (2005). *Modern theory and practice*. Chapman and Hall/CRC.

Choudhury, K. S., & Kishore, K. G. (1991). *Role of the life insurance corporation in economic development of India*. Himalaya Publishing House.

Cummins, D., & Venard, B. (2007). *Handbook of international insurance between global dynamics and local contingencies*. Springer.

Das, N. G. (1990). *Statistical methods in commerce, accountancy & economics (Part-1)*. M. Das & Company.

Desai, V. (2005). *Financial system and development innovative success*. Himalaya Publishing House.

Gaur, A. S., & Gaur, S. S. (2011). *Statistical method for practice and research*. Response Books.

Gujarati, D. N., Porter, D. C., & Gunasekar, S. (2012). *Basic econometrics*. McGraw Hill Education Private Limited.

© The Author(s), under exclusive license to Springer Nature Singapore Pte Ltd. 2022
S. P. Patra et al., *Investment Pattern of LICI and Select Private LICs in the Post-reforms Era in India*,
https://doi.org/10.1007/978-981-19-2799-7

Gupta, A. (2003). *Insurance: A general text book.* Cyber Tech Publications.

Haridas, R. (2011). *Life insurance in India.* New Century Publication.

Kanji, G. K. (2006). *100 statistical test.* Sage.

Khan, M. Y. (2006). *Indian financial system.* Tata McGraw Hill Publishing Company Limited.

Kothekar, R. (2011). *Perspective on life insurance.* Cyber Tech Publications.

Kulkarni, M. V. (2008). *Marketing research.* Everest Publishing House.

Kumar, D. (1991). *Tryst with trust: The LIC story.* LIC of India.

Malhotra, N. K. (2006). *Marketing research an applied orientation.* Prentice Hall of India Private Limited.

Makridakis, S. C., Wheelwright, S., & Hyndman, R. J. (2005). *Forecasting methods and applications.* Wiley & Sons Inc.

Palande, P. S., Shah, R. S., & Lunawat, M. L. (2003). *Insurance India changing policies and emerging opportunities.* Response Books.

Pathak, B. V. (2006). *The Indian financial system.* Pearson Education.

Plantin, G., & Rochet, J. C. (2007). *When insurers go bust—An economic analysis of the role and design of prudential regulations.* Princeton University Press.

Saha, S. S. (2013). *Indian financial system and markets.* Tata McGraw Hill Education Private Limited.

Sharma, R. (2010). *Insurance.* Lakshmi Narain Agarwal.

Shrivastawa, R. K., & Upadhyay, Y. (2007). *Risk management in banking and insurance.* Deep and Deep Publications Private Limited.

Sinha, A., & Gandhi, S. K. (2014). *Financial performance analysis of life insurers in India.* Scholar's Press.

Skipper, H. D., & Jean, K. W. (2007). *Risk management and insurance perspectives in a global economy.* Blackwell Publishing.

Trivedi, P. R. (2008). *Encyclopaedia of insurance business and management.* Janada, Prakashan.

Upadhyay, Y., & Shrivastawa, R. K. (2007). *Risk management in banking and insurance.* Deep & Deep Publication Private Limited.

Vanderhoof, I. T., & Altman, E. I. (1998). *The fair value of insurance liabilities.* Kluwer Academic Publishers.

JOURNAL ARTICLES

Adams, M., & Hardwick, P. (2003). Actuarial surplus management in United Kingdom life insurance firms. *Journal of Business Finance and Accounting,* 1–14.

Anand, S. (2014). Insight quarterly newsletter. *NFIFWI, 2*(3).

Bala, N., & Sandhu, H. S. (2011). Analysis of factors influencing agents' perception towards Life Insurance Corporation of India. *International Journal of Industrial Marketing,* 1–23.

Bawa, S. K., & Chattha, S. (2013). Financial performance of life insurance in Indian insurance industry. *Pacific Business Review International*, 1–9.

Bedi, H. S., & Singh, P. (2011). An empirical analysis of life insurance industry in India. *International Journal of Multidisciplinary Research*, 1–12.

Chandra, S. C., & Ramesh, J. (2011). Lapsing of policies in life insurance sector-need for competitive strategies. *Journal on Banking Financial Services & Insurance Research*, 1–14.

Chandrapal, J. D., & Brahmbhatt, A. C. (2015). Evaluation of life insurance industry in India-past and present—An overview. *Asian Journal of Research in Business Economics and Management*, 1–9.

Chandrasekaran, R., Madhanngopal R., & Kartik, K. (2013). A stochastic frontier model on investigating efficiency of Life insurance Companies in India. *International Journal of Mathematics Trends and Technology*, 1–9.

Charumathi, B. (2012). On the determinants of profitability of Indian life insurers—An empirical study. *Proceedings of the World Congress on Engineering*, 1–6.

Das, M., Lalremtluangi, C., Atwal, S., & Thapar, S. (n.d.). A study on risk return characteristics of life insurance policies. *SSRN*, 1–25.

Das, B., & Mohanty, S. (2008). Mutual fund VS. life insurance: Behavioural analysis of retail investors. *International Journal of Business and Management*, 1–15.

Diamond, J. M., & Henebry, K. L. (1998). Life insurance company investment portfolio composition and investment regulations. *Journal of Insurance*, 1–22.

Dickinson, G. (2011). Encouraging a dynamic life insurance industry: Economic benefits and policy issues. *City University Business School of London*.

Ege, L., & Bahadir, T. (2011). The relationship between insurance sector and economic growth: An econometric analysis. *IJER*, 1–12.

Gopalakrishana, D. (2010). The philosophy of life insurance. *The Journal of Insurance Institute of India*, 36, 75–81.

Gour, B., & Gupta, M. C. (2012). A review on solvency margin in Indian insurance companies. *International Journal of Recent Research and Review*, 1–5.

Henebry, K. L., & Diamond, J. (1998). Life insurance investment portfolio composition and investment regulations. *Journal of Insurance Issue*, 1–22.

Horton, J., & Macve, R. (1998). Planned changes in accounting principles for UK life insurance companies: A preliminary investigation of stock market impact. *Journal of Business Finance & Accounting*, 1–33.

Jain, R. (2014). Insurance: An investment opportunity & tool for risk management (A comparison between Individual Assurance and Pension Plans of LIC). *Pacific Business Review International*, 1–5.

Koijen, R. S. J., & Yogo, M. (2013). The cost of financial frictions for life insurers. *SSRN.COM/abstract=2031993*, 1–50.

Kumari, T. H. (2013). Performance evaluation of Indian life insurance industry in post liberalization. *International Journal of Social Sciences Arts and Humanities*, 1–8.

Kumar, V., & Kumari, P. (2012). A comparative study on public VS private sector in life insurance. *VSRD International Journal of Business and Management Research*, 1–3.

Lee, C. C., Lee, C. C., & Chiu, Y. B. (2013). *The link between life insurance activities and economic growth: Some new evidence*, 1–23.

Mahdzan, N. S., & Victorian, S. M. P. (2013b). Determinants of life insurance demand: A focus on saving motives and financial literacy. *Canadian Centre of Science and Education*, 1–11.

Nagarajan, G., Asif, A., & Sathyanarayana, N. (2013). A study on performance of unit-linked insurance plans (ULIP) offered by Indian private insurance companies. *International Journal of Advanced Research in Management and Social Sciences*, 1–14.

Negi, D., & Singh, P. (2012). Demographic analysis of factors influencing purchase of life insurance products in India. *European Journal of Business and Management*, 1–13.

Nena, S. (2013). Performance evaluation of Life Insurance Corporation (LIC) of India. *International Journal of Advance Research in Computer Science and Management Studies*, 1–6.

Niwata, N. (1971). The economic theory of insurance and social security, 37–68.

Noronh, M. R. (2012). A comparative study of cost efficiency of life insurance companies in India. *GFJMR*, 1–14.

Padhi, B. (2013). Role & performances of private insurance companies in India, in the post liberalization era. *International Journal of Engineering, Business and Enterprise Applications*, 1–7.

Panda, B. N., & Panda, J. K. (2012). A factorial analysis of mutual fund investment and insurance fund investment: A comparative study. *Journal of Business Management, Commerce & Research*, 1–11.

Rai, A., & Medha, S. (2013). The antecedents of customer loyalty: An empirical investigation in life insurance context. *Journal of Competitiveness*, 1–25.

Rajendran, R., & Natarajan, B. (2009). The impact of LPG on life insurance corporation of India (LIC). *Asia Pacific Journal of Finance and Banking Research*, 1–12.

Saad, N. M., & Idris, N. E. H. (2011). Efficiency life insurance company in Malaysia and Brunei: A comparative study. *International Journal of Humanities and Social Science*, 1–12.

Satpathy, S., & Sahoo, R. (2012). Effectiveness of executives—A comparison between different insurance sectors. *VSRD International Journal of Business & Management Research*, 1–6.

Shreedevi, D., & Manimegalai, D. (2013). A comparative study of public and private non-life insurance companies in India. *International Journal of Financial Management*, 1–8.

Singh, H., & Singh, P. (2011). An empirical analysis of life insurance industry in India. *International Journal of Multidisciplinary Research*, 1–12.

Verma, A., & Bala, R. (2013). The relationship between life insurance and economic growth: Evidence from India. *Global Journal of Management and Business Studies*, 1–10.

WEBPAGES

Aegon Religare Life insurance Company. *About history of company*. Retrieved from AEGONRELIGARE Website: http://www.aegonreligare.com

Aviva Life Insurance Company. *About history of company*. Retrieved from AVIVAINDIA Website: http://www.avivaindia.com

Bajaj Allianz Life Insurance Company. *About history of company*. Retrieved from BAJAJALLIANZ Website: http://www.bajajallianz.com

Bharti AXA Life Insurance Company. *About history of company*. Retrieved from BHIRTIAXALIFE Website: https://www.bharti-axalife.com

Birla Life Insurance Company. *About history of company*. Retrieved from Insurance BIRLA SUNLIFE INSURANCE Website: http://insurance.birlasunlife.com

Breusch-Pagan Test. *Homoscedasticity*. Retrieved from KELLOGG Website: http://www.kellogg.northwestern.edu

Breusch-Pagan Test. *Res-1 & Pre_1*. Retrieved from KELLOGG Website: Prehttp://www.kellogg.northwestern.edu

Companies Act. *Indian Companies Act, 1883*. Retrieved from SHODHGANGA Website: http://shodhganga.inflibnet.ac.in

Company Act. *Indian Insurance Company Act, 1928*. Retrieved from ICPR Website: http://www.icpr.itam.mx

DHFL Pramerica Life Insurance Company. *About history of company*. Retrieved from DHFLPRAMERICA Website: https://www.dhflpramerica.com

Durbin-Watson Test. *Static ranges*. Retrieved from UTEXAS Website: http://www.utexas.edu

Durbin-Watson Test. *Statistic value*. Retrieved from HELPSAP Website: http://help.sap.com

Edelweiss Tokio Life insurance Company. *About history of company*. Retrieved from EDELWEISSTOKIO Website: http://www.edelweisstokio.in

Exide Life Insurance Company. *About history of company*. Retrieved from EXIDELIFE Website: http://www.exidelife.in

Future Generali India Life Insurance Company. *About history of company*. Retrieved from FUTUREGENERALI Website: http://www.futuregenerali.in

HDFC Life insurance Company. *About history of company.* Retrieved from HDFCLIFE Website: http://www.hdfclife.com

History of LICI. *About LICI.* Retrieved from LICI India Website: https://www.licindia.in

ICICI Prudential Life Insurance. *About history of company.* Retrieved from ICICIPRULIFE Website: http://www.iciciprulife.com

IDBI Federal Life Issuance Company. *About history of company.* Retrieved from IDBIFEDERAL Website: http://www.idbifederal.com

Independent Samples t-Test. *Test using SPSS.* Retrieved from STATISTICS Website: https://statistics.laerd.com

India First Life Insurance Company. *About history of company.* Retrieved From INDIAFIRSTLIFE Website: http://www.indiafirstlife.com

Insurance Law Bill. *Amendment bill, 2015.* Retrieved from INDIANBARASSO-CIATION Website: https://www.indianbarassociation.org

Insurance Laws. *Amendment bill, 2015.* Retrieved from INDIANBRASSOCIA-TION Website: https://www.indianbarassociation.org

Insurer Regulations. *About IRDA.* Retrieved from SHODHGANGA Website: http://shodhganga.inflibnet.ac.in

Kotak Mahindra Old Mutual Life Insurance Company. *About history of company.* Retrieved from INSURANCE KOTAK Website: http://insurance.kotak.com

Life Insurance Act. *Indian Insurance Companies Act, 1928.* Retrieved from ICPR Website: http://www.icpr.itam.mx

Life Insurance Company. *Overview of life insurance company.* Retrieved from SHODHGANGA Website: http://shodhganga.inflibnet.ac.in

Life Insurance Corporation Bill. *Amendment bill, 2009.* Retrieved from BILL-TEXTS Website: http://164.100.47.4/billstexts/lsbilltexts/PassedBothHouses/LIC.

Life Insurance Industry. *Entry of private life insurance players.* Retrieved from IRDA Website: https://www.irdai.gov.in

Life Insurance Industry. *Name of life insurance company.* Retrieved from IRDA Website: www.irdai.gov.in

Max Life Insurance Company. *About history of company.* Retrieved from MAXLIFEINSURANCE Website: http://www.maxlifeinsurance.com

Mobilization of Savings. *Risk coverage.* Retrieved From CCI Website: http://www.cci.gov.in/images/media/ResearchReports/IntRepShilpa280311.pDF

Multicollinearity. *Tolerance & VIF.* Retrieved from STATISTICSSOLUTION Website: http://www.statisticssolutions.com

Obligation of Insurer. *IRDA regulations, 2000.* Retrieved from IRDA Website: https://www.irdai.gov.in

Obligation of Life Insurance. *IRDA act, 1999.* Retrieved from IRDA Website: https://www.irdai.gov.in

Overview of Life Insurance Company. *Brief study*. Retrieved from SHOD-
HGANGA Website: http://shodhganga.inflibnet.ac.in

Paired t-Test. *Test using SPSS*. Retrieved from STATISTICS Website: https://sta
tistics.laerd.com

PNB MetLife India Insurance Company. *About history of company*. Retrieved
from PNBMETLIFE Website: http://www.pnbmetlife.com

Reliance Life Insurance Company. *About history of company*. Retrieved from
RELIANCELIFE Website: http://www.reliancelife.com

Sahara India Life Insurance Company. *About history of company*. Retrieved from
SHODHGANGA Website: http://shodhganga.inflibnet.ac.in

SBI Life Insurance Company. *About history of company*. Retrieved from SBILIFE
Website: http://www.sbilife.co.in

Shriram Life Insurance Company. *About history of company*. Retrieved from
SHRIMLIFE Website: http://www.shriramlife.com

Star Union Dai-Ichi Life Insurance Company. *About history of company*. Retrieved
from SUDLIFE Website: https://www.sudlife.in

Tata AIA Life Insurance Company. *About history of company*. Retrieved from
TATAAIA Website: http://www.tataaia.co

Total Investment of LICI. *Annual investment*. Retrieved from PLANNING-
COMMISSION Website: http://planningcommission.nic.in

Wikipedia. *Levene's test*. Retrieved from WIKIPEDIA Website: https://en.wikipe
dia.org

Wikipedia. *Methodology of Levene's test*. Retrieved from WIKIPEDIA Website:
https://en.wikipedia.org

Wikipedia. *Methodology of Shapiro Wilk test*. Retrieved from WIKIPEDIA Website:
https://en.wikipedia.org

Wikipedia. *Shapiro Wilk test*. Retrieved from WIKIPEDIA Website: https://en.
wikipedia.org

Wikipedia. *Unit linked plan*. Retrieved from WIKIPEDIA Website: https://en.
wikipedia.org

URLs

http://planningcommission.nic.in
www.irdai.gov.in
www.rbi.gov.in
www.lici.in

Databases

Handbook on Indian Insurance Statistics, 2011–2012.
Handbook on Indian Insurance Statistics, 2014–2015.

IRDA, Annual Report, 2004–2005.
IRDA, Annual Report, 2005–2006.
IRDA, Annual Report, 2006–2007.
IRDA, Annual Report, 2007–2008.
IRDA, Annual Report, 2008–2009.
IRDA, Annual Report, 2009–2010.
IRDA, Annual Report, 2010–2011.
IRDA, Annual Report, 2011–2012.
IRDA, Annual Report, 2012–2013.
IRDA, Annual Report, 2013–2014.
IRDA, (Investment) Regulations, 2000.
IRDA, (Investment) (Amendment), Regulations, 2001.
IRDA, (Investment) (Amendment), Regulations, 2013.

INDEX

A

Adjusted R^2, 110, 153

Administrative Reforms Commission (ARC), 26

Aegon Religare Life Insurance Company Ltd.
capital contribution, 30
collaboration of, 30

All India National Congress (AINC), 25

All Indian Life Assurance Offices Association (AILAOA), 23, 24

Analysis of growth, 9, 70, 72, 73, 81, 160

Analysis of significant difference, 162

Analysis of trend, 8, 71, 72, 83, 91, 161

Approved investment (AI), 4, 56–58, 64, 65, 77, 81, 82, 93, 99, 103, 104, 106, 110, 113, 115, 116, 120, 121, 138–141, 144, 146–151, 153, 154, 158, 160, 161, 165

growth, 81, 83
trend, 91, 93, 95

The Assurance Companies Act, 1909, 21

Augmented Dickey-Fuller (ADF) test, 6

Aviva Life Insurance Company Ltd.
current capital, 30
customers, 30
joint venture between, 30
shareholding, 30

B

Bajaj Allianz Life Insurance Company Ltd. (BAJAJ)
capital contribution, 30
joint venture between, 30
premium collection
growth, 73–75
trend, 86, 87
sector-wise investment
growth, 77

trend, 91
total investment
    growth, 75–77
    trend, 89
Bharat Insurance Company, 22, 23
Bharti AXA Life Insurance Company
    Ltd.
    capital contribution, 31
    collaboration of, 31
    products, 31
    shareholding, 31
Birla Sun Life Insurance Company
    Ltd. (BIRLA)
    capital contribution, 31
    joint venture between, 31
    premium collection
        growth, 73–75
        trend, 86, 87
    sector-wise investment
        growth, 77
        trend, 91
    total investment
        growth, 75–77
        trend, 89
Bombay Insurance Company Ltd, 22
Bombay Mutual Life Assurance
    Society Ltd, 22
British Insurance Act, 1870, 22

C
Canara HSBC Life OBC Life
    Insurance Company Ltd.
    capital contribution, 31
    joint venture of, 31
Central Government market securities,
    59, 61, 63
Chi-square, 117, 118
Committee of actuaries, 26
Compounded Annual Growth Rate
    (CAGR), 10, 84, 86–91, 93,
    95–97, 106, 161

Correlation
    among LICs
        approved investment, 103
        infrastructure investment, 101
        investment in government and
            other approved securities,
            101
        other than approved
            investment, 104, 105
        premium collection, 99
        total investment, 99
    between total premium and total
        investment, 96
Correlation analysis, 71, 72, 96, 161
Cowasji Jehangir committee, 24

D
Data Envelopment Analysis (DEA), 6
Degree of freedom, 111
Dependent variable (DV), 84, 110,
    112, 113, 115, 125, 144, 147,
    150, 152, 164
DHFL Pramerica Life Insurance
    Company Ltd.
    capital contribution, 32
    joint venture of, 32
Dunn-Bonferroni test, 109

E
Edelweiss Tokio Life Insurance
    Company Ltd.
    capital contribution, 32
    joint venture between, 32
Empire of India Life Insurance
    Company Ltd., 22, 23
The Equitable Life Assurance Society,
    21
Era Sezhiyan committee, 26, 62, 63
Evolution of Life Insurance Industry
    Indian scenario
        post-independence era, 24–26

post-reforms era, 27
pre-independence era, 22, 24
pre-reforms era, 27
World scenario, 20, 21
Exide Life Insurance Company Ltd.
  channels of distribution, 32
  distribution relationships, 32
  equity capital, 32

F

Financial institutions, 2, 4, 10, 35
  functions, 2
Financial market, 2, 4, 8, 11, 28, 55, 77
Financial system, 2, 4, 7, 10
  role, 2
  sub-systems, 2
Foreign life insurance companies, 27, 41, 45
F-test, 6, 8, 10, 110, 153
Future Generali India Life Insurance
  Company Ltd.
  capital contribution, 33
  joint venture between, 33

G

Games-Howell test, 109, 118, 163
General insurance company, 15, 165
Global economic recession
  premium collection, 106, 108, 109, 125, 154, 162, 163
  sectorial investments
    approved investment, 104, 106
    infrastructure investment, 4, 104, 160
    investment in government and other approved securities, 4, 99, 104, 110, 160
    other than approved investment, 104, 106

total investment, 104, 106, 108, 109, 125, 162, 163
Government of India Marketable
  Securities, 60
Government securities, 25, 56–58, 64, 65
Grouping of Individual Companies, 163

H

HDFC Standard Life Insurance
  Company Ltd. (HDFC)
  capital contribution, 33
  joint venture between, 33
  life insurance products, 33
  premium collection
    growth, 73–75
    trend, 87
  sector-wise investment
    growth, 77
    trend, 91
  shareholding, 33
  total investment
    growth, 75–77
    trend, 89
Heteroscedasticity, 115
Homogenous subsets
  premium collection, 108, 109
  sectorial investments, 108, 109
  total investment, 108, 109, 117, 123
Homoscedasticity, 109, 111, 114, 125–129, 132–134, 137–144, 146, 162, 163
Hypothesis, 97, 111, 114–118, 122, 126, 127, 129, 131, 133, 137, 139–141, 146, 149, 150, 153

I

ICICI–Prudential Life Insurance
  Company Ltd. (ICICI)

asset under management (AUM), 34
capital contribution, 34
joint venture between, 34
premium collection
    growth, 73–75
    trend, 86, 87
sector-wise investment
    growth, 77
    trend, 91
shareholding, 34
total investment
    growth, 75–77
    trend, 89
IDBI Federal Life Insurance Company Ltd.
    foreign and Indian equity capital, 34
    joint venture among, 34
    network, 34
    sum assured of all the products, 34
Impact
    industry performance, 106, 108, 147–151, 154, 155, 162, 164
    ownership structure, 109, 110, 143–147, 162, 163
    recession, 106, 108, 125, 127–132, 134–144, 154, 162, 163
Independent sample t-test, 15, 109, 110, 125, 128, 134, 140, 144
Independent variable (IV), 84, 110, 112, 113, 147, 150, 164
IndiaFirst Life Insurance Company Ltd.
    capital contribution, 34
    shareholding, 34
Indian Companies Act, 1866, 23
Indian Insurance Companies Act, 1928, 23, 41
Indian Life Insurers
    brief overview, 28
    linked products, 29

micro-products, 29
non-linked products, 29
offices, 29
Industrial policy of 1990, 43
Informal Group constituted by the Central Government, 60
Infrastructure Investment (II), 4, 64, 79, 99, 101–104, 110–112, 115, 117, 122, 123, 134, 138, 144–151, 153–155, 158, 164
    growth, 77, 79, 80, 106, 160, 161
    trend, 91–94
Insurance
    history, 7, 21, 22, 33, 35, 65, 160
    principles, 8, 22, 39, 49
    risk management, 6, 7, 166
Insurance Act, 1938, 7, 24, 27, 41–43, 46, 49, 54–56, 58, 59, 159
Insurance Act, 1950, 25, 44, 57
Insurance company, 2–7, 9–15, 20–25, 27, 28, 30, 31, 34, 35, 39, 40, 42, 43, 45–47, 52–58, 64–66, 70–73, 75, 77, 79, 81, 93, 96, 99–105, 144, 158–160, 165–167
Insurance industry, 3, 5, 7, 9–11, 20, 25, 28, 43, 46, 53–55, 57, 64, 70, 147, 158, 166
    future prospect, 7, 11
    influence of global market on growth, 7, 11
The Insurance Law (Amendment) Bill, 2008, 51
Insurance Laws (Amendment) Bill, 2015, 46, 51, 53
Insurance Ombudsmen, 54
Insurance Regulatory and Development Authority of India (IRDAI)
    developmental roles, 47
    functions, 46

regulations, 3, 11, 46, 47, 49, 58
Insurance Regulatory Authority
   (IRA), 43
Insurance sector, 2, 6, 7, 9, 24,
   38–40, 44, 46, 53, 166
reforms, 160, 165, 166
Insurance service, 8
Interactive Voice Response System
   (IVR), 30
Investment in government and other
   approved securities (IGOAS), 3,
   4, 99–102, 110–112, 114–116,
   118, 120, 132, 134, 135,
   144–151, 153–155, 158, 164,
   165
growth, 77, 78, 104, 161
trend, 91, 92
Investment institutions, 2
Investment portfolio
   post-independence nationalisation
      era, 56, 58, 59
   post-reforms era, 7, 12, 27, 58, 66,
      70, 160
   pre-independence era, 55, 56, 64,
      160
   pre-reforms era, 5, 58, 65
   relationship among the LICI and
      select private LICs, 5, 12
   trend, 5, 70–72
IRA Bill, 1996, 43
IRDA Act 1999, 160
IRDA (Assets Liabilities and Solvency
   Margins of Insurance)
   Regulations, 2000, 50
IRDA Bill, 1998, 43
IRDA (Insurance Advertisement and
   Disclosure) Regulations, 2000,
   49
IRDA (Investment) (Fifth
   Amendment) Regulations, 2013,
   53

IRDA (Investment) Fifth Amendment
   Regulations, 2015, 4
investment portfolio, 4
IRDA (Issuance of Capital by Life
   insurance Companies)
   Regulations, 2011, 52
IRDA (Licensing of Banks as
   Insurance Brokers) Regulations,
   2013, 53
IRDA (Life Insurance-Reinsurance)
   Regulations, 2013, 52
IRDA (Obligation of Insurer to Rural
   or Social Sector) Regulations,
   2000, 48
IRDA (Preparation of Financial
   Statements and Auditors Reports
   of Insurance Companies)
   Regulations, 2000, 49
IRDA (Protection of Policyholder's
   Interest) Regulations, 2002, 51
IRDA (Standard Proposal Form for
   Life Insurance) Regulations,
   2013, 52

J
Jagannathan committee, 61
Janata Policy Scheme, 25
Judgment sampling method, 13

K
Kotak Mahindra Old Mutual Life
   Insurance Company Ltd.
   joint venture between, 35
   promoters, 35
   shareholding, 35
Kruskal-Wallis (K-W) test, 162

L
Level of significance, 97, 111, 114,
   116, 117, 122, 128, 132, 150,
   153

Levene's test, 114, 115, 126, 127, 129, 131, 133, 135, 137, 139–141, 143, 146, 162
LICI Act, 1956, 46
  modifications, 58
Life Assurance Act, 1774, 21
Life assurance societies, 21
Life fund, 24, 25, 27, 28, 45, 46, 55, 56, 58, 64–66, 160
Life insurance
  density, 4, 167
  determinants of demand, 6
  nationalisation, 3, 7, 25, 27, 45, 58
  penetration, 4, 27, 53, 57, 66, 159, 167
  premium collection, 4, 8–10, 13, 70–75, 77, 96–100, 104, 108–110, 147, 160, 164, 165
Life insurance business
  development, 7, 8, 26
  performance, 8, 10, 27
  products, 9, 27
Life Insurance Companies (LICs)
  efficiency and technical changes, 6
  historical evolution, 12
  impact on stock market, 5
  investment portfolio, 5, 55, 58, 70
  private, 3–5, 9, 11–13, 15, 27, 28, 66, 70–73, 75, 76, 104, 108, 160
  public, 3, 4, 9, 11, 12, 24, 28
  regulatory framework, 20
  savings mobilisation, 11
Life Insurance Companies Act, 1912, 23, 39
The Life Insurance Corporation (Amendment) Bill, 2009, 51
Life Insurance Corporation of India Limited (LICI)
  changing policy, 7
  competition faced, 8
  date of formation, 35

individual assurance and pension plan, 10
investment committee, 59, 63
investment policy 1958, 26
investment strategy, 8
market share, 4, 9, 104, 152, 160, 166
performance, 8, 66, 149, 154, 155, 158, 163, 164, 166
premium collection
  growth, 73, 74
  trend, 87
sector-wise investment
  growth, 77
  trend, 91
total investment
  growth, 75, 76
  trend, 89
Life Insurance Council, 47
  objectives, 54
Life Insurance (Emergency) Provisions Act, 1956, 25
Life insurance industry
  customer loyalty, 9
  influence of LICI, 5
  influence of select major private LICs, 5
  investment portfolio, 55, 58, 158
  operating efficiency, 9
  other laws, 54
  performance during pre- and post-recession era, 8
Life Insurance Ordinance, 1956, 25
Life insurance organisation, 4
Life insurance policy, 21, 51
Life insurance sector, 3, 4, 8–11, 27, 39, 41–43, 45–47, 54, 55, 58, 65, 66, 75, 109, 110, 125, 159, 164
  impact of LICI, 109, 110
  impact of PLICs, 109, 110

Life insurer, 21, 27, 28, 36, 39, 41,
    46–48, 52, 54, 57, 74, 104, 110,
    117, 118, 122, 143, 146,
    165–167
  financial friction, 6
  investment portfolio, 4, 27
Loans on policies, 61, 62
Loans to National Housing Bank, 59
Log-linear model, 15, 105, 161

M

Malhotra committee, 43, 58, 160
Mann-Whitney (M-W) test, 109, 110,
    129–132, 163
Mararka committee, 26
Marine insurance, 20, 22
Max Life Insurance Company Ltd.
    (MAX)
  customer service, 35
  joint venture between, 35
  premium collection
      growth, 73–75
      trend, 87
  promoter, 35
  sector-wise investment
      growth, 77
      trend, 91
  total investment
      growth, 75–77
      trend, 89
Mean, 9
MetLife India Insurance Company
    Ltd. (MetLife India)
  capital contribution, 36
  joint venture among, 36
  life insurance products, 36
  shareholders, 36
Model fitness, 110
Mortality Table, 21
Multiple linear regression analysis
    (MLRA), 15, 110, 147, 148,
    152, 164

Mundhra scandal, 25

N

Nayudu committee, 26
Nippon Life Insurance Company, 36
  foreign and Indian equity capital,
    36
Normality, 109, 110, 125, 126,
    128–130, 132–134, 136–141,
    144–146, 162, 163

O

One-way analysis of variance
    (ANOVA), 7, 15, 109–113, 117,
    162, 163
Oriental Government Security Life
    Assurance Company, 23
Oriental Life Insurance Company, 22
Other investment, 6, 56, 58, 59, 64
Other than approved investment
    (OAI), 4, 64, 65, 81, 84, 96, 99,
    104–106, 110, 111, 115, 117,
    118, 122–124, 140, 143–150,
    152–155, 158, 160, 162–165
  growth, 77, 81, 84, 85
  trend, 91, 93, 94, 97, 98
Ownership structure, 154
  impact of
      premium collection, 109
      sectorial investments, 109, 110
      total investment, 109, 110

P

Pair-wise difference
  approved investment, 120
  infrastructure investment, 123
  investment in government and
      other approved securities, 120
  other than approved investments,
      123

premium collection, 119
total investment, 122
Parameter estimates, 110
significance, 110
Pearson's correlation coefficient, 15,
    72, 97, 99, 106, 161
Pension and annuity fund, 58, 65, 66,
    160
Pension, general and group fund, 55
PNB MetLife India Insurance
    Company Ltd., 36
Population variance, 114, 115, 125,
    127, 131, 135, 137, 140, 143,
    145, 146
Post hoc test, 109, 118, 163
Premium mobilisation, 5, 11, 15, 65,
    71, 159, 166
growth, 74
trend, 71
Private life insurance companies
    (PLICs)
insurance premium mobilisation,
    12, 13, 15, 70
investment portfolio, 3, 5, 9, 11,
    12, 15, 70–72
performance, 9, 66, 154, 158, 164
role, 9
total investments, 4, 13, 70–72, 75,
    76, 104, 106, 108–110, 117,
    152, 154, 158, 160–162
total life insurance premium
    collection, 13
Private sector investment, 62
Probability value, 99, 112–124,
    126–128, 130–132, 134–147,
    151–154
Public life insurance companies, 3, 4,
    9, 11, 12, 24, 28

R
Ramanathan committee, 26

Redressal of Public Grievances Rules,
    1998, 54
Reliance Nippon Life Insurance
    Company Ltd., 36

S
Sahara India Life Insurance Company
    Ltd.
products, 37
total capital, 37
venture of, 37
SBI Life Insurance Company Ltd.
    (SBI)
authorised capital, 37
collaboration between, 37
distribution channels, 37
partners, 37
premium collection
    growth, 73–75
    trend, 87
sector-wise investment
    growth, 77
    trend, 91
shareholding, 37
total investment
    growth, 75–77
    trend, 89
Secondary data, 14, 15, 71, 72
Sectorial investments
approved investment, 149
growth, 104, 105, 160, 161
infrastructure investment, 4, 160
investment in government and
    other approved securities, 99,
    104, 110, 160
other than approved investment,
    106
trend, 91, 105, 161
Securities and Exchange Board of
    India (SEBI), 43, 52, 54
Shapiro-Wilks (S-W) test, 111, 162

Shriram Life Insurance Company Ltd.
  capital, 37
  joint venture between, 37
Significant difference
  among LICI and select PLICs
    premium collection, 106, 108, 162
    sectorial investments, 108, 162
    total investment, 162
Socially oriented sectors, 60, 61, 63
Standard deviation (SD), 116
Standard error, 118
Standardised coefficients, 149
Star Union Dai-ichi Life Insurance Company Ltd.
  capital, 38
  joint venture of, 38
  shareholding, 38
State Government securities, 60–63
Stochastic frontier analysis (SFA), 10
Strength of association, 97, 110, 147, 150, 152–154
Sum of squares, 150
Swadeshi Movement, 23, 39

T
Tata AIA Life Insurance Company Ltd.
  joint venture between, 38
  partners, 38
  shareholding, 38

Test statistic, 97, 111, 114, 117–119, 122–124, 127, 128, 131, 150, 153
Thaper committee, 26
Total insurance premium, 13
Total investment, 10, 13, 66, 75, 96–101, 104–106, 108–110, 123, 128–132, 147, 148, 150, 151, 155, 160–162, 164, 165
  growth, 71, 72, 75–77
  trend, 88–90
Tukey's Honestly Significant Difference (HSD) test, 109
Two-way ANOVA, 8

U
Unit linked fund, 55, 58
Unit Linked Products (ULIPs), 4, 11, 30, 31, 33, 53, 64–66, 159, 160

W
Welch-Satterthwaite equation, 116
Welch's test, 109, 115, 162

Y
Year-wise Growth Analysis, 15, 72
Yogakshema, 21

Z
Z-statistic, 122
Z-test, 8

Printed in the United States
by Baker & Taylor Publisher Services